NAVIGATING THE

INTERIOR LIFE

30 DAYS WITH

TERESA OF AVILA

Bordon

1) Madejs ✓
   Ritosas ✓
   Burlings ✓

2) Nelsons ✓
   Agosti ✓
   Urbancics ✓
   ~~Rodriquez~~ ✓
   Humphreys ✓
   Smith ‑
   Reynolds ✓

3) Reeds ✓
   Shivelys ✓
   Wostowskis ✓
   Yates
   Bruenings
   Payne ‑
   Loxterman
   Martin
   Saxton ✓
   Stiemles
   ‑ R Geraci
   ‑ MacKay?

Navigating the Interior Life

Interior Life

30 Days with

Teresa of Avila

WITH AN INTRODUCTION AND
REFLECTIONS BY
DANIEL BURKE AND ANTHONY LILLES

Navigating the Interior Life: 30 Days with Teresa of Avila was previously published by Emmaus Road Publishing, 827 North Fourth Street, Steubenville, Ohio 43952.

Original cover design by Claudia Volkman and cover layout by General Glyphics, Inc.
Printed in the United States of America.

Sophia Institute Press
Box 5284, Manchester, NH 03108
1-800-888-9344

www.SophiaInstitute.com

Sophia Institute Press® is a registered trademark of Sophia Institute.

TABLE OF CONTENTS

INTRODUCTION

To understand the letters of Teresa of Avila, we need to look at them as a vital part of one of the greatest of enterprises taken up in sixteenth-century Spain. For those who know this time period, this is saying a lot, but it is not hyperbole. Her letters are evidence that the Carmelite reform that Teresa helped to pioneer was at the heart of a broader renewal of the practice of mental prayer throughout Spain.

Contemplative prayer is an encounter with God ordered to the most beautiful and powerful experimental knowledge. A profoundly personal and existential kind of knowing, it raises one's whole existence to a supernatural level from the deepest center of one's being to the furthest extent of is psychological powers, from the most wondrous dispositions of heart to the most wholesome and tender of human acts. At once an intellectual and an affective engagement in the self-disclosure of the Holy Trinity, this effort to be vulnerable to the highest degrees of mystical prayer is ordered to the glory of God and the perfection of Christian holiness in the life of the Church.

This renewal was ignited in the Benedictine Abbey of Montserrat under the Abbot Cisneros, himself a great mystic. The conversion of St. Ignatius of Loyola is also attached to this place of prayer and conversion. Sts. John of Avila and Peter of Alcantara fanned these same flames so that Francis Borgia, John of God, and a veritable army of Franciscan, Jesuit, and Dominican priests not only preached the importance of mental prayer but spread a deep devotion to prayer into the New World. The greatest discoveries of the sixteenth century may not be limited to the new geographic territories and peoples, but must include the even vaster and unfamiliar horizons of divine Love.

If what she and her contemporaries found surprises us today, it is only because—even after two thousand years of exploration—the inexhaustible riches of Christ constantly offer us something new, so that more exquisite wonders await those who will follow her trail into the living splendors of God. Teresa of Avila is an explorer par excellence, a pioneer, a guide to this divine world that is at once ever ancient and ever new.

In these letters, we find Teresa of Avila implicating everyone in this adventure of prayer and self-giving to God—from the mighty King of Spain to an anxious cloistered nun, from her blood relatives to her new brother and sisters in religion. She has advice for everyone, and at the same time, she relies on them. They are on a dangerous mission together: she leads them across the waves and storms of all kinds of interior and exterior trials, around traps laid by political intrigue and potential for self-deception, and straight into a life and death struggle with the titanic cultural forces of her time and demonic powers of darkness.

In each letter, her charm and powers of persuasion are unleashed to provide a word of hope, a pathway forward, sometimes even a little gentle correction, but most of all a little refreshment to her fellow-weary pilgrims. The spirit of solidarity we find between the lines of these spiritual gems suggest that she found the same encouragement from them, that they were together, united in the new work Christ was accomplishing in His Mystical Body.

These humble reflections on the letters of this spiritual giant are not meant as a last word or a definitive statement on her project. These brief meditations on her private words to her friends are meant to encourage a deeper and more prayerful reading of these beautiful texts. Because her letters were unedited and produced more or less on the fly as she had time to respond, she introduces ideas and teachings that she will refine in her major writings, especially *The Interior Castle*. Where there is sometimes less precise use of terminology, she still provides an authentic witness and good practical advice concerning the gift of mystical contemplation in the life of the Church. Our hope is to provide just enough orientation to the spiritual and historical context of the letter that it will surrender its spiritual riches to those who want to sit with us at the feet of this great Doctor of the interior life.

DAY 1

XV
Valladolid, December 28, 1568[1]
To Doña Inès Nieto, at Madrid
On the admission of a postulant into
the recently founded convent at Valladolid.
JESUS!
May the grace of the Holy Spirit be with you!

ALTHOUGH I have not written before, you may be sure that I have not forgotten you in my poor prayers to our Lord and that I shared your happiness. May He permit you to enjoy it in His service for many years, for I hope your happiness will not impede this service, whatever obstacles may arise. For the so-called goods of this miserable life are impediments, and your having spent your past years for God will have repaid you by teaching you to estimate things rightly and so to care nothing for what is fleeting. . . .

Your unworthy servant,
Teresa de Jesus, Carmelite

Reflection

Detachment: Ever growing union with God consists both in an elevation of the entire person through contemplative wisdom, and a cleansing of the heart through detachment. Detachment is:

---

1. Teresa of Avila, *The Letters of Saint Teresa*, trans. Benedictines of Stanbrook (London: Thomas Baker, 1919), vol. 1. Excerpts from a longer letter. Hereafter: *Letters*, vol. 1.

the withholding of undue affection for creatures for the sake of the Creator. When mortal sin is involved, detachment is imperative for salvation. Detachment from creatures that are an obstacle to complete service of God is a normal condition for growth in holiness.[2]

The "undue affection" of attachment is simply a disordered occupation of the heart. Not every movement of heart is noble, and many ignoble attachments can cause us to betray ourselves and those who are counting on us, especially God Himself. Any loving, desiring, or clinging to some person, place, or thing that is not purely for the glory of God renders the soul incapable of giving that same love to God or others to whom, for the glory of God, it is owed. At the same time, precisely because our affections are misdirected, we are not as open or vulnerable to the blessings that God might otherwise desire to pour out on us.

Because God, in a certain sense, relies on our faithfulness to Him and His loving plan for us, we have an obligation to order our affections in accord with His wisdom for our lives. It is a matter of saving our strength and internal resources for the Lord and His purposes. It is a matter of letting go of our own whims and earthly dreams to make room in our hearts for heavenly things and the will of the Father.

The great mystic recognizes that Dona Ines Nieto has a difficult lesson to learn. Teresa herself came to estimate material things rightly only after many difficult setbacks in her own walk with Christ. It is always futile and a waste of energy to place one's security in anything that is not God. The Saint knows that even one's own happiness can become an obstacle, an impediment. Indeed, every form of self-satisfaction blocks us from receiving even greater blessings than we might otherwise know.

This kind of wisdom comes many ways. To some, it comes through physical or emotional suffering, others the traumatic experience of the death of a loved one, and still others the deep sadness that invades the

---

2. Fr. John Hardon's *Modern Catholic Dictionary*.

heart when what is desired is gained but fails to satisfy the desire that only God can satisfy. The answer? Shed as much as we can as quickly as we are able. Give to anyone who asks. Love nothing in this life but God. Pursue only God and His will. This is the only hope of true and lasting peace in this life, and joy in the ascent to God.

DAY 2

XVII
Valladolid, February 19, 1569[1]
To Alonzo Ramirez
Cause of the delay in the journey to Toledo.
Encouragement in the difficulties likely to arise.
JESUS!

As REGARDS the licenses, with the help of heaven I hope to get the king's easily. There may be a certain amount of worry about it, as I know by experience that Satan cannot endure our houses and always persecutes us, but God is all-powerful and the evil one goes off with a broken head.

We had a great deal of trouble here from the leading men of the city but it is all over now. Do not suppose that you will have to offer God no more than you have planned; you will have to give Him much more. He rewards good works by sending us an opportunity for greater ones. It is nothing to give coppers—they cost us little—but when people stone you and your son-in-law and all of us who have taken part in the matter (as they nearly did in Avila when St. Joseph's was founded), then the project will succeed, and I believe that neither the convent, nor we who suffer in the cause, will be any the worse for it, but will gain greatly. May God direct the whole affair as He sees best! Do not feel at all anxious. . . .

Your unworthy servant,
Teresa of Jesus, Carmelite

---

1. Teresa of Avila, *Letters*, vol. 1, excerpts.

Reflection

Spiritual Warfare: One can almost see a smirk on the face of Teresa as she writes the last line of this paragraph, "Do not feel at all anxious." After letting her victim know that he will have to give far more than he is prepared to give, and reflecting on the devil's response to the advance of the kingdom, she seems to find a bit of fun in the battle.

Teresa was ever aware of the work of the enemy in and through people. But she was even more aware of the strength of God's kingdom as it advances: "Satan cannot endure our houses."

Many rightly quote Matthew 16:18 when speaking of the battle we face as we advance the kingdom of God:

> *And I tell you, you are Peter, and on this rock I will build my Church, and the gates of Hades shall not prevail against it.*

However, the common interpretation is often far from the meaning of Jesus' words. He proclaims that He will build His Church on the confession and ordination of Peter, and that the gates of hell will not be able to hold back the advance of the kingdom as it breaks in and invades territory otherwise occupied by the enemy.

The mighty warrior mystic knows firsthand the proper interpretation of Jesus' words in this passage. She rightly sees the establishment of her monasteries as an assault and occupation of enemy territory. As such, as when a beehive is disturbed, she also knows the consequences and the heavenly rewards as she reveals in *The Way of Perfection* chapter 38:

> I feel convinced that souls which have arrived at this degree of perfection in prayer do not ask God to deliver them from trials or temptations, nor from persecutions and combats. This is another unmistakable and noteworthy effect, showing that the contemplation and favors given to such people come from the Holy Ghost and are not illusions, for, as I said just now, these souls wish for and demand such troubles and love them instead

of hating them. They are like soldiers—the more they fight, the better they like it, for thus they hope for a richer booty. When there is no war they live on their pay, but they know they will not grow rich on that. Believe me, sisters, the battle never comes soon enough for the soldiers of Christ. I allude to contemplatives, and people who practice prayer. They have little fear of open enemies, knowing them well already and being aware that such foes have little power against the strength given them by God through which they always gain the victory and come forth from the fray with great spoils and riches, so that they never beat a retreat.

With this faith-filled conviction and an extraordinary strength of will, she unhesitatingly disturbs the hive knowing she will be stung, but that the suffering—rather than weaken her—will only make her stronger and further establish the work of God in her heart and in her mission.

Her comfort comes not from any human ability to endure the assault, but from knowing that God is working in and through the assault, and that by her "yes" and His grace, she will conquer all the territory that He assigns to her.

DAY 3

XIX
Toledo, March 1569[1]
To Doña Maria de Mendoza
Letter of condolence. The foundation at Toledo.
JESUS!
May the Holy Spirit be with you!

I HAVE made this journey with a very heavy heart, for I deeply regretted leaving Valladolid after receiving a letter from his Lordship the Bishop stating that you were undergoing a severe trial, although not explaining what it was. Had it not come on the eve of my departure, I would not have left you in such trouble; however, it has had the great advantage of leading me to pray much to our Lord for you. I do not know why I fancy that your trial may be connected with the Administrator's opposition to the Lady Abbess. The idea consoled me, for although it would be a cross, God might permit it for the benefit of her soul. May it please His Majesty to dispose of matters as I beg of Him!

I was very glad to hear that your health is excellent. Oh, if only your self-control equaled your control over others, how little would you care for the world and all its troubles! . . .

Thank God you set them so good an example. And how do you think you must do so now? By bearing the many crosses by which our Lord begins to fan the love for Him which He has lit in your soul in

---

1. Teresa of Avila, *Letters*, vol. 1, excerpts.

order that it may enkindle others. So that I entreat you to take courage: think of what our Lord suffered at this time. Life is short; our trials last but a moment. . . .

Your Ladyship's unworthy servant and subject,
Teresa de Jesus, Carmelite

Reflection

"Life is short, our troubles last but a moment": These words reflect a great spiritual principle that is important to meditate on often in our service to the Lord. Without knowing the details of the circumstances surrounding this letter, we know that St. Teresa had already faced many trials and hardships. It had been a little more than ten years since she fell on her knees before a statue of the humiliated Christ "Ecce Homo," begging Him to give her the grace not to backslide.

She had already begun to realize the power of God at work in mental prayer to make all things new. The renewal of the Carmelite charism and the renewal of the Church required a re-dedication to contemplative prayer. One would not think that something as beautiful and simple as deepening one's devotion to prayer would upset anyone or that pursuing this would meet with any objection. The Lord, however, allows His work as well as those He loves to be purified and strengthened by all kinds of testing and trials.

When, at that time, she felt the Lord call her to the particular vocation of starting a reform of contemplative life, St. Teresa could never have imagined the trials she would face. Even less could she have guessed the trials that those who collaborated with her would have to endure. She stood in solidarity with them: she was distressed by anything that caused them distress. At the same time, she bore these trials with a contagious hope because she bore them all with love.

By the hope she had in God, she knew that such distress was not really an obstacle to the work of reform or even a threat to contemplative prayer. Instead, hardship, trials, setbacks, disappointments, betrayals, and all kinds of other necessary sacrifices were the pathway forward. She knew this because she had already grasped that the success of the reform would not be realized by clever tactics and strategies, but instead by love alone.

Mental prayer and the contemplative vocation are all about love at the center of the Church, and the only love that is really worth anything is that which is disciplined by trials and spent in sacrifice.

Love has its own law of gravity: hardships born in love and for love only fan love's flames, drawing others to its warmth and light. Love patiently rises above hardship and all kinds of persecution, even in what seem to be insurmountable circumstances and crushing setbacks. Love does not need to force circumstances or control situations, but makes use of everything, even failures and inadequacies. Even the open hostility of others furthers love's hidden purpose, implicating everyone in a deeper solidarity of misery and mercy, of prayer and penance, and, most of all, of holiness and hope.

When we go to serve the Lord, there are bound to be all kinds of trials. If we want our marriages to work, or we want to put the Lord in the center of our family life, or if we desire to renew the devotion of our communities, we must expect great trials as we turn to the Lord in prayer.

How can our love be great if there is no trial, no testing, if everything comes too easy? How important it is to remind ourselves that the secret of serving the Lord has so little to do with the success of the programs we are involved in!

It has even less to do with the personal agendas we bring into our households and communities, no matter how pious our intentions. The secret of witnessing to the presence of the Lord instead is love. In our own day, as Blessed Teresa of Calcutta observed, we cannot love except at our own expense.

DAY 4

XLII
Avila, circa September 14, 1572[1]
Reply to a spiritual challenge of the
friars and nuns at Pastrana.
JESUS, MARY!

ON READING the challenge, we thought we could not brace ourselves to encounter in the field such mettlesome and puissant knights. For no doubt they would conquer us and leave us rifled of all our goods—we might even be so daunted as to leave undone the little that was in our power. Therefore not one of us took up the gauntlet—least of all Teresa de Jesus—and this is the simple truth.

We agreed to try our strength and perhaps, when we have practiced the art, with the goodwill and help of those who wish to meet us in the fray, we may be able, in a few days, to sign the challenge.

Yet this must be on condition that our assailant does not turn his back and shut himself up in a hermitage, but descends to the arena of the world we live in. Perhaps, when he finds the fighting is incessant, that he cannot lay down his arms, stand off his guard, nor take a single moment's rest in safety, he will not be so warlike, for there is all the difference between words and deeds as we have some reason to know.

Let him sally forth! Let him and his comrades leave their peaceful life! Perhaps, when they have gone a little way and begin to stumble

---

1. Teresa of Avila, *Letters*, vol. 1, complete letter.

and fall, they will need our aid to rise, for it is terrible to be in constant danger, weighed down with arms, with nothing to eat. Since the quartermaster has such store of rations, let him send us what he promised without delay, for it would win him little profit or glory to starve us out.

Every knight or daughter of our Lady who daily asks God to keep sister Beatriz Juarez in His grace, that she may always speak deliberately and for His glory, will receive in return her merits gained by two years' attendance on extremely tiresome invalids.

Sister Ana de Bergas says that if the knights and sisters will beg God to remove a certain difficulty and to grant her humility, she will give them all the merits she gains if their prayers are answered.

The Mother Subprioress, whose name is Isabel de la Cruz, declares that if these cavaliers pray that she may renounce self-will, she will give them all her merits for two years.

To any of these knights who gazes on a crucifix three times a day in honor of the three hours our Lord hung on the Cross, and obtains for her the victory over a strong passion which torments her soul, Sister Sebastiana Gomez promises all the merit she wins by its conquest.

To all who recite a *Pater Noster* and *Ave Maria* daily to obtain for her patience and resignation in her ill-health, Mother Maria de Tamayo offers, on each day that they pray for her, the third part of the merits won by her sufferings which are excessive: for more than a year she has been unable to speak.

Sister Ana de la Miseria promises to the knights and daughters of the Blessed Virgin who, while contemplating the poverty in which Jesus Christ was born and died, shall demand for her the poverty of spirit which she has vowed to His divine Majesty, that she will bestow on them all the reward she earns in the sight of God by grieving over her sins committed in His service.

To all the squires and daughters of the Virgin who shall watch beside our Savior for the three hours in which He hung living on the Cross, and who shall obtain for Sister Isabel de Santangelo grace to keep her three vows perfectly, she offers a share in the sufferings her soul has gone through.

Sister Beatriz Remon declares that she will give a year of the merits she gains to each friar or daughter of the Virgin who begs God daily to grant her humility and obedience.

Sister Maria de la Cueva makes over three years of her merits (which are no slight ones, for she has passed through severe interior trials) to every knight or daughter of our Lady who shall daily ask for her the gift of faith, light, and grace.

Sister Maria de San José proffers a year of her merits to those of the above mentioned religious who entreat our Lord to make her humble and obedient.

To anyone who begs our Lord for the gift of self-knowledge for Sister Catalina Alvarez, she will give what she has earned by a year of sufferings, which means a great deal.

For any cavalier or sister who will intercede with our Lady to obtain from her Son grace for Sister Leonar de Cantreras to serve God and to persevere, she will recite three times daily the *Salve Regina*—so it will be well to pray for her every day.

If any knights or daughters of the Blessed Virgin will daily ask our Lord to bestow His love on Sister Ana Sanchez, she will daily recite for their intentions three *Ave Marias* in honor of our Lady's purity.

Sister Maria Gutierrez offers a share in all her merits in God's sight to anyone who prays that she may obtain a perfect love for God and may persevere in it.

Sister Maria Cimbron says that those who pray for her happy death will participate in what she gains by her sufferings. For a long while she has been unable to move in bed, and her end is near.

Sister Inés Diaz will recite five times daily the *Pater Noster* and *Ave Maria* for those who ask each day that she may share what the Virgin felt at the foot of the Cross.

If the above mentioned knights and sisters will beg our Lord to make Juana de Jesus contrite for her sins, she offers them part of the many humiliations and sufferings brought on her by her misdeeds of which the number is large.

To those above mentioned who ask our Lord, for the sake of the torture He suffered when the nails were driven into His flesh, to grant Sister Ana de Torres grace to serve Him and to obey, she pledges whatever merits she may gain this year.

To anyone who will ask of Christ, in memory of what He endured while being nailed to the Cross, that grace may be given Catalina Velasco not to offend Him and that our Order may increase, she will devote part of what she obtains during the time she spends daily at our Lady's feet, which means a great deal.

To those who will obtain for her patience, humility, and light to serve God, Sister Jeronima de la Cruz will say the *Credo* thrice daily, and will bestow what her past sufferings have gained during a year. But they must perform their part every day.

A 'free lance' declares that if the Commander of the forces will obtain for him from God the grace required to serve Him perfectly in all that obedience requires, the said 'free lance' will give in return all the merits obtained by such service during the year.

For those knights and daughters of the Virgin who ask our Lord that Sister Estefania Samaniego may serve Him and may never offend Him, and that He may give her living faith and gentleness, she will recite daily the prayer *O bone Jesus*! and will give them the merits won during a year by her sufferings and temptations in the past.

Sister N. de la Gila pledges the third part of the merits gained by her suffering and illnesses during her life to all knights and daughters of the Virgin who will recall daily for a few minutes our Lady's sorrows and will beg her help (of which Sister N.'s soul stands in great need), and also that the life of our Mother Prioress, Teresa de Jesus, may be prolonged for the benefit of our Order.

To any of the knights of the Virgin who will once daily make a firm resolution to bear during his whole lifetime with a superior who is extremely foolish, vicious, gluttonous, and ill-tempered, Teresa de Jesus offers half of what she merits on that day, both by receiving Holy Communion and by the many pains she suffers—and after all, it will not amount to much. The knight must meditate upon our Lord's humility before His judges and how He was obedient unto death.

This contract is binding for the next six weeks.

Reflection

In Weakness God's Power is Made Perfect: The knights and ladies of Our Lady referred to throughout this strange letter are none other than Carmelite friars and nuns. This is in fact a famous response to a spiritual challenge offered in jest, but even more, in love.

The friars of Pastrana had written out a formal challenge, in something like the style of the Spanish Royal Court. St. Teresa and the nuns of the Incarnation were challenged to match their penances as if they were squaring off with each other in mortal combat. This original document, in accord with the knightly code of the time, required signatures of acceptance. It was of course meant as a witty encouragement to heroic Lenten practices. In response, Teresa of Avila issues her own challenge, and with it, a little spiritual wisdom.

Her response is completely light-hearted, but not light-minded. Adroitly veiling her rejection of their challenge under the pretext of intimidation, she changes the battlefield and introduces her own spiritual taunts. She does not feel capable of entering onto the battlefield of great spiritual exploits. Instead, she invites the friars down into the world where she and her cloistered nuns struggle incessantly: the arena of real life. She is teasing in good fun when she challenges the friars to "Sally forth," but the constant vigilance and dangerous difficulties of living vulnerably and humbly before God that she presents here are no laughing matter.

Our solidarity with one another in the Church is a solidarity of weaknesses, and this requires not only bearing with one another patiently but, most of all, a lot of prayer for and with each other. Notice how St. Teresa indirectly identifies foolish and ill-tempered superiors with herself and counts her own sufferings (that were in fact very great) as of so little account.

The free lance (or knight-errant) refers to St. John of the Cross who is spiritual director at the Monastery of the Incarnation at this time. The friars proposed a challenge that would test one another's spiritual strength. Teresa wrote an invitation to share in one another's weaknesses and frailties. Sister after sister is listed, not according to their spiritual achievements, but according to their spiritual poverty. In fact, some of them are dying.

If the friars will help the nuns by praying for them, the nuns agree to share the gifts that Christ gives them as a result. Such is the communion of the saints, a communion of frailty and blessing, because it is through our mutual love for one another that the glory of God is revealed.

DAY 5

XLVII
Convent of the Incarnation, Avila. June 4, 1573[1]
To His Sacred, Imperial, and Catholic Majesty,
the King Our Seigneur
St. Teresa informs King Philip II that the
Carmelite Order is praying for him; she asks a favor.
JESUS!
May the grace of the Holy Spirit ever be with your
Majesty! Amen.

I FEEL sure that your Majesty is aware that I persevere in recommending you to our Lord in my poor prayers. And although, considering what a wretched creature I am, it is rendering you but little service, yet I do you some good by inciting the Discalced nuns to pray for you, as I know that they serve God faithfully. The community in this convent intercedes for your Majesty, for our Lady the Queen, and for the Prince, to whom may God grant a very long life. Special prayer was offered on the day on which the oath of allegiance was tendered to his Royal Highness. As we shall persevere in our petitions, your Majesties will benefit by the growth of our Order. I therefore venture to beg your Majesty to support us upon certain points which the licentiate Juan de Padilla will notify to you. I leave the matter to him and ask your Majesty to credit his word. His zeal is such that I have entrusted the affair entirely to him, as if it became public, the object for which we are striving, which is solely for the honor and glory of God, would be defeated. May the

---

1. Teresa of Avila, *Letters*, vol. 1, complete letter.

divine Majesty preserve you for many years as the welfare of Christendom requires! In these days of trials and persecutions, it is a great consolation that God should have provided for the Church such a valiant defender and aid as your Majesty.

From the Convent of the Incarnation, Avila.
Your Majesty's unworthy servant and subject,
Teresa de Jesus, Carmelite

Reflection

Intercessory Prayer: St. Teresa's commitment to intercessory prayer for the leaders of her time was both reflective of a primary personal concern for their souls and also for the practical realities of the need for wise leaders.

Phillip II, whom she addresses here, understood the importance of the contemplative vocation and was devoted to building a genuinely Christian society in Spain. With brilliant daring and at great personal cost, Phillip II had been staunch in promoting the faith both inside and outside the Church. Shortly before Teresa wrote this letter, Phillip turned back an Islamic naval invasion at the Battle of Lepanto, but now faced a second naval assault. In northern Europe, he had recently quelled an iconoclastic rampage, but heterodox zealots were now preparing a violent rebellion. In other words, Teresa is promising her prayers to a leader whose plans have gone amiss even though he was committed to doing everything for the honor and glory of God.

Instead of criticizing or abandoning him, she stands in solidarity with him in prayer. This solidarity is not based on a passive wish: open to a real mutual concern, this prayerful love compels her to invite him to aid her efforts to promote a way of life rooted in mental prayer. The intercessory prayer that comes out of this kind of life is the path to peace and communion, not because of an absence of conflict, but in spite of it. In fact, the renewal of mystical prayer that Spain comes to enjoy under Phillip II is arguable one of the most perduring achievements of his reign.

Teresa's heart clearly mirrors the heart of God who is concerned about all our plans and failures, personal and social. He not only wants us to know His faithfulness when we are under fire, but He also invites us into ever greater works, even as our own plans seem to be falling apart. Her prayer and confident invitation are in perfect harmony with St. Paul's admonition in his first letter to Timothy:

> *First of all, then, I urge that supplications, prayers, intercessions, and thanksgivings be made for all men, for kings and all who are in high positions, that we may lead a quiet and peaceable life, godly and respectful in every way. This is good, and it is acceptable in the sight of God our Savior, who desires all men to be saved and to come to the knowledge of the truth. (1 Tim 2:1–4)*

If we, like St. Teresa, wish to daily live in peace with respect to our civil leaders, we must bear in our hearts this same commitment to pray for them diligently and regularly, while not failing to find ways to invite them to take part in the greater works God is accomplishing in the world.

DAY 6

XLVIII
Convent of the Incarnation, Avila[1]
To Father Ordoñez, S.J., Medina Del Campo
Concerning the foundation at Medina by Elena de Quiroga of a girls' school connected with the nuns, and the entrance of her daughter Geronima into the convent.
JESUS!
May the grace of the Holy Spirit ever be with you!

I WISH I had time and strength to discuss certain matters with you which I consider important, but my health has been unspeakably worse since the messenger left than before. It will cost me dear to say what I can, and being so unequal to the task I am sure to be tedious, however brief I try to be. This convent of the Incarnation evidently injures my health; God grant I may gain some merit by it!

I am more anxious than ever now that this matter seems almost settled, especially since reading the letter today from the Father Visitor, who leaves the affair entirely to me and to the Father Master Domingo to whom he has written, delegating all his own powers to us. I always feel nervous when any decision is left to me, being sure that I shall go utterly wrong. True, I have laid the matter before God as has this community.

It seems to me, my Father, that we must look well at all the drawbacks to the project, for if it turns out ill, no doubt God and the world will lay the blame on us. Therefore, never mind about a delay of a fort-

---

1. Teresa of Avila, *Letters*, vol. 1, excerpts.

night or so. I was very glad to learn from your letter that the Prioress is only concerned with the two matters you mention. Believe me, it is highly important, as you say, that one good work should not be sacrificed to another.

The idea of taking pupils in the way you mention has always been repugnant to me, for I know well that a number of girls are as different from boys to teach as black is from white. The obstacles to doing any good in a large girls' school are too many to mention here. It would be best to fix the number of pupils, which when over forty is far too large and results in nothing but confusion. The children disturb one another and no good can come of it. I am told that thirty-five is the limit at Toledo and no more can be received. I assure you that so many girls and so much noise are in every way undesirable. If some people will give no alms because the number is small, then go on by degrees: there is no hurry. Make your community holy and God will help it; we must not injure the work for the sake of gifts. . . .

Your unworthy servant and daughter,
Teresa de Jesus

Reflection

Illness and Suffering: St. Teresa faced persistent illness most of her life. She often verbalizes her struggles, though she admonishes her sisters to do as little of this as is necessary. Even so, she rarely yields to the physical challenges she faces. Instead, she simply informs her superiors or others of her limitations and battles through her suffering to fulfill her mission.

The fuel behind her strength to fight through these struggles is rooted in her acute awareness of her participation with Christ in her suffering for the sake of all. She is also aware of the strength of will and faith that increases when we fight the temptation to yield, or to be thwarted or discouraged by our suffering. Teresa's heart resonates with St. Peter's perspective on suffering as revealed in his first letter to the exiles:

In this you rejoice, though now for a little while you may have to suffer various trials, so that the genuineness of your faith, more precious than gold which though perishable is tested by fire, may redound to praise and glory and honor at the revelation of Jesus Christ. Without having seen him you love him; though you do not now see him you believe in him and rejoice with unutterable and exalted joy. As the outcome of your faith you obtain the salvation of your souls. (1 Pet 1:6–9)

Discernment: Because God delights in the response of human freedom in love, this life is filled with a kind of necessary ambiguity and uncertainty. Seeking God's will through prayer and careful consideration redeems this ambiguity (even if it doesn't remove it). It does so by helping us to discover just the amount of certitude we need to serve Him in the most appropriate way. There are spiritual principles that help us in this effort and St. Teresa presents a very important one here: "Make your community holy and God will help it."

When it comes to the work of sanctification in our families and communities, it is possible to place too much importance on the many gifts God gives us. We can even become preoccupied with whether or not we have the financial, physical, or psychological resources we need to do good things for God. Teresa speaks into this anxiety and invites us to renounce it. Our concern must be first and foremost the work of our mutual sanctification. Everything else needs to be ordered towards this end or we are likely to be deceived into inaction.

Humility: One of the more beautiful aspects of St. Teresa's character is her humility. Though she is obviously an intellectually strong and holy woman, a woman capable of navigating political and social situations with an unusual wisdom, she is always ready to reveal her weaknesses and sin. In fact, some of her works were originally edited because they were so self-effacing. However, this self-deprecating quality has a very powerful effect on her readers as it helps us to realize that saints are real people.

In this letter, she openly reveals her anxiety and nervousness about the decisions and demands she faces. Yet she does so with an unyielding and steely determination to do God's will. She reveals this same bold humility in the thirty-eighth chapter of 'The Way of Perfection' when she says,

> There is another temptation. When God gives us some virtue, we must understand that it is only a loan and that He may take it away again, as indeed often happens, not without a wise providence. Have you never found this out yourselves, sisters? I certainly have. Sometimes I fancy that I am very detached, as I really am when it comes to the trial. Yet at another time I discover that I am so attached to things which I should perhaps have laughed at the day before, that I hardly know myself. Again, I feel such courage that there is nothing I should fear to do in God's service, and I find, when it comes to the proof, that I am brave sometimes—yet, next day, I should not venture to kill an ant for Him if I met with any opposition. Sometimes I care nothing if people talk or complain of me; and indeed very often it has even given me pleasure. Yet there are occasions when a single word disturbs me and I long to leave this world, for everything in it disgusts me. I am not the only person to whom this happens, for I have noticed it in people better than myself, and I know that it is a fact.[2]

Authentic humility—bold humility—never shirks or shrinks from the call of God. Instead, it recognizes its own weakness and its true source of strength and insistently takes hold of that Source in faith as it flails headlong into the dark call of God.

---

2. Teresa of Avila, *The Way of Perfection*, 2nd ed. (London: Thomas Baker, 1919), 234–35.

DAY 7

LIV
Salamanca, December 3, 1573[1]
To the Father Master Domingo Bañez, Valladolid
The Saint's loneliness. Advice for Mother Mary Baptist.
JESUS!

. . . I ASSURE you, my Father, that I think my joys are no longer of this world, for I have not got what I want and I do not want what I have. My trouble is caused by my no longer being able to find comfort in my confessors—it must come from something higher than a confessor, for nothing that is less than the soul itself can satisfy its desire. It has been a great relief to tell you this—God grant you may always find relief in loving Him! Tell that insignificant little person, who is so very much concerned as to whether the nuns will vote for her or not, that she interferes too much and is wanting in humility, for both you and we who have the welfare of the convent in view are more interested than the sisters in the choice being a good one. It is truths of this kind that nuns must be made to understand.

Remember me most kindly to Señora Doña Maria when you see her, for it is a long time since I wrote to her. It is a great mercy that her health should be better in such bitterly cold weather. I believe that today is December 3.

Your Reverence's daughter and servant,
Teresa de Jesus

---

1. Teresa of Avila, *Letters*, vol. 1. The beginning of this letter is missing.

Reflection

Detachment: The more deeply we grow in the interior life, the less need we have of earthly consolations—those good feelings we get from having even the positive or pleasurable things that are worthy of having in this life.

This process of denudation begins with detachment from material wants and needs, and typically lessens our hold on places, things, and even people. Though we continue to love and appreciate people (always more deeply than before), we no longer need them. Instead, we love with a more pure love that has little self-interest or benefit.

Often in this process we begin to cling to pieces of heaven provided us here on earth: our time in prayer and the sacraments, our spiritual directors, our retreats and holy objects. But ultimately, even these things fail to bring us comfort as our hearts yearn for the ultimate reality that all of these created things lead us to, and that ultimate uncreated reality is God Himself.

Sometimes the absence of consolation in creation (even in the hearts of holy people) can cause distress. This distress comes in the form of aridity, loneliness, and other manifestations of a kind of longing. But when we understand the reasons behind this longing, we know, as St. Teresa knows, that we are ready to be tested in true love—a love that seeks nothing other than the will of the Beloved.

Only in this more perfect self-giving do we find some sense of true satisfaction that in some way mirrors the complete reality we will know in eternity. However, our longing will never be completely satisfied until we see Him face to face—until we fully love and we are fully loved because we "know as we are fully known" (1 Cor 13:12).

DAY 8

LX
Segovia, beginning of June 1574[1]
To Antonio Gaytan, Salamanca
Advice about prayer. The foundation at Segovia.
JESUS!
May the Holy Spirit be with you, my son!

I AM not lucky enough to have time to write you a long letter as I am sure I wish that I could. I am delighted to hear from you and learn how God bestows greater blessings on you every day. He is rewarding you for what you did for us here.

Do not tire your brain by trying to work it during meditation. I have often told you what to do; perhaps you may remember. It is a higher grace from God that you should continually praise Him and wish that others should do so too, and a striking proof that your mind is fixed on Him. May He be pleased to teach us both how to repay part of what we owe Him and may He give us much to suffer for Him—if only from fleas, ghosts, and bad roads.

Antonio Sanchez was ready to let [give] the house without further discussion, but what were you and Father Julian thinking about when you wanted to buy such a place? It was fortunate that the owner would not sell it. We are about to purchase one near St. Francis' church, in the Calle Real, the best of the suburbs and near the market. It is a very

1. Teresa of Avila, *Letters*, vol. 1, complete letter.

good house. Will you kindly pray about it. I am better—I was about to say I am well, for to have nothing beyond my usual ailments is very good health for me. May God give you good health and have you in His keeping for us!

Your servant,
Teresa de Jesus

Reflection

Mental Prayer: Here, St. Teresa repeats a teaching on mental prayer and meditation that is found in each of her major works.

She admonishes her reader to avoid overtaxing his mind during mental prayer. She is oft quoted as saying that "the good of the soul does not consist in its thinking much, but in its loving much."[2] Some mistakenly take this to mean that thoughts during prayer are to be avoided or to be "let go" of. However, she clearly contradicts this view in the fourth chapter of *The Interior Castle* where she admonishes her readers to avoid methods aimed at emptying the mind of thoughts.

Instead, she is counseling against an unhealthy preoccupation with what we think or feel in prayer. She is aware that the Holy Spirit burns with love in the devoted soul even when our thoughts and imagination do not seem to cooperate with Him. Here, the effort to be vulnerable to the presence of God can be frustrated when we dissipate ourselves on trying to control our thoughts. It is a question of surrender and trust. The intellect and the imagination can sometimes work against our efforts to pray. They act like energetic children who do not know how to behave before the Lord. But once the love of God has captured us and begins to burn in our hearts, struggling to vanquish thoughts and imaginings is a waste of time and energy.

---

2. Teresa of Avila, *The Book of the Foundations of S. Teresa of Jesus*, trans. D. Lewis (London: Thomas Baker, 1919), 39.

Instead, prayer becomes the simple effort of patiently awareness of the Lord's presence in the midst of our own brokenness. St. Teresa is not surprised that we face distractions in prayer, but invites our merely natural and psychological efforts to a completely new loving attentiveness made possible by the indwelling of the Holy Spirit.

DAY 9

LXI
Segovia, June, 1524[1]
To Antonio Gaytan
Counsels him about prayer and advises him to consult Father Baltasar Alvarez.

MAY JESUS be with you and repay you for your gift of a book, which is just what I want!

I should require more time than I have to answer your question about prayer. On the whole you behave as people usually do who have attained to contemplation: I have told you so several times as you may perhaps remember. In fact, the state of the soul varies like the weather; it could not be otherwise: do not distress yourself about it for it is no fault of yours.

As to the rest, I am no judge, being a special pleader. I naturally prefer solitude, though I do not deserve to enjoy it. As it is also the spirit of our Order, I might counsel you according to my own liking and not to your advantage. Lay the subject clearly before the Father Rector who will know what is best for you, and be guided by the inclinations of your soul. God be with you! I have written so many letters that I do not know how I managed to say as much as this, and the messenger is waiting.

Nothing can be settled about my journey nor do I know how it can take place this year. However, God can do all things.

1 .Teresa of Avila, *Letters*, vol. 1, complete letter.

Pray much for me as I do for you, and write to me often.

Your unworthy servant,
Teresa de Jesus

Reflection

Spiritual Direction: St. Teresa is a deeply insightful spiritual director. As she demonstrates most profoundly in *The Interior Castle*, she has a keen intuitive sense regarding what is normal and abnormal in various phases of spiritual growth. Here she demonstrates clarity regarding the changes and struggles in a soul that *is* gifted with contemplative prayer. She affirms the reality of this work of God in Fr. Alvarez.

Teresa reassures Fr. Alvarez regarding the authenticity of his prayer, just as others had done for her. Her own experiences of spiritual growth made her aware of the full gambit of spiritual weather that a soul suffers in prayer from storms of scrupulosity and difficult droughts where devotion is want.

Her counsel is transcendent and simple: instead of attending to the soul's weather conditions, she attends to the Lord who is above the weather. The real messiness of spiritual progress can be an occasion for frustration, but the involuntary vacillation of the Godward heart, even aided by grace, is all part of the normal way God brings a soul into spiritual maturity.

What she wants him to recognize is consummately practical: a soul never progresses toward union with God as in climbing up a ladder with clearly distinct mechanical steps. Because the Lord wills to reveal His power in our weakness, growth in contemplative prayer requires great patience with one's own humanity, a patience that comes not from surmounting one's frailties, but rather in offering these to God in love. This means that mood swings, fluctuations in pious affections, boredom and even struggles with distractions do not ultimately define our prayer, if through it all we never lose trust in God.

The love of God unfolding in the heart that prays is greater than all interior movements either voluntary or involuntary. The prayer of faith attends to this love and believes in it more than one's own inadequacies, voids, and failures. The great Spanish mystic is convinced that prayer animated by such faith establishes a soul in a kind of peace that can weather any storm.

The great Carmelite Foundress and Reformer is particularly wise in recognizing that a spiritual director should never attempt to force a directee into the former's preferred or professed spirituality. In this case, Fr. Alvarez was a Jesuit priest with a very distinct spirituality that St. Teresa seems keen to avoid disrupting. As well, during this time there was some tension within the Society of Jesus regarding mental prayer over which she desired to avoid stirring up contention.

The wisdom of discernment requires obedience to the spiritual authority of another and a mutual awareness of the noble desires moving in one's heart. We might surmise that the priest writing her is concerned about how much time he should spend in silent prayer. One might think that the answer would be the more the better. St. Teresa, doctor of the Church though she is, is more deliberative and careful.

Good discernment requires a certain transparency and an acceptance of ambiguity and vulnerability of heart. Here, good spiritual directors never assume that they can help everyone that seeks their advice. Teresa is humble and reverent before the mysterious ways the Lord works. She wisely points Fr. Alvarez in the direction of a Rector whom she feels might more appropriately assist him. At the same time, she also invites him to be cognizant of the desires of his heart.

May we all be blessed with such wisdom as we seek out one of the most powerful gifts for growth in union with God: spiritual direction.

DAY 10

LXIII
Segovia, June, 1574[1]
To the Most Illustrious
Señor Don Teutonio de Braganza, Salamanca
Congratulations on his safe return. The Saint's health.
Confirmation of the Apostolic Visitors.
Projected foundation of a priory at Salamanca.
JESUS!
May the grace of the Holy Spirit be with your Reverence!

THE NEWS that you are well was very welcome and a great comfort to me. But after so long a journey, yours seemed a very short letter and you do not even tell me whether the object of your expedition was attained.

It is nothing new for you to be discontented with yourself, but do not be distressed if the fatigues of your travels and the disturbance of your ordinary routine should make you feel rather tepid: peace of body will restore peace of soul. . . .

Your Lordship's unworthy servant and subject,
Teresa de Jesus, Carmelite

Reflection

Aridity: Feeling "tepid" as St. Teresa notes is akin to feeling lukewarm or even experiencing spiritual aridity. It can also refer to a sense

---

1. Teresa of Avila, *Letters*, vol. 1, excerpts.

of being out of tune, scattered, and unable to recollect oneself in prayer. Often this state can originate in very simple causes that are easy to identify or eliminate.

It is always wise to first look to natural causes before exploring elsewhere for answers to this potentially frustrating experience. Sometimes, time off from work, a few good nights of longer rest, or a retreat to silence can restore the soul to a state of peace that was lost to the bane of fatigue, busyness and the incessant noise of modern living.

The state of our physical bodies, how much sleep we have had, how well we are feeling, fatigue and illness, often have significant impact on our spiritual or psychological health and resilience. Like Teresa we can, by the grace of God, often push through these difficulties and even use them to the benefit of our spiritual growth and that of others through redemptive suffering. However, in this case, she prudently recommends rest.

Because it can interrupt our discipline of prayer, we should also be on guard against any travel that is not for the glory and honor of God. In fact, developing and sticking to a good routine in our prayer life (this can also be called a plan of life) helps us stay more recollected and focused on the Lord. Sometimes after travel, before we return to our routine, it is also very important to take the time we need for physical rest.

"Peace of body will restore peace of soul." This wise phrase is worthy of frequent consideration by those of us who tend to push ourselves to our physical limits.

DAY 11

LXIV
Segovia, July 3, 1574[1]
To Don Teutonio de Braganza, Salamanca
The Saint rejects a title of honor. The foundation at
Segovia. Trials of prayer. Father Pedro Hernandez.
JESUS!
May the grace of the Holy Spirit be with your Lordship!

I DECLARE that if you address me again by such a title I will not answer your Lordship. I do not know why you wish to inflict on me the pain such titles always give me, although I never felt it so keenly as I have today. Inquire of the Father Rector how to style me[2]; what you wrote is entirely opposed to the spirit of our Order. I am glad to hear that he is in good health, as I was anxious about him. Will you kindly remember me to him.

This seems to me a very unsuitable season in which to begin your cure. God grant it may succeed, as I pray that it may! May His Majesty also grant a safe journey to your attendants. But I wish you were not so concerned about the matter. How can that benefit your health? Oh! If we only realized such truths, how few things on earth would trouble us!

I sent your letters at once and wrote to the Father Rector, telling him that it was important for the affair to be settled immediately. I owe

---

1. Teresa of Avila, *Letters*, vol. 1, complete letter.
2. To "style me": how to address letters to me. Teresa does not want to be addressed in a way descriptive of another kind of living and status that fails to adequately reflect the humble spirit of poverty, chastity, and obedience of the Order—Editor.

much to him: he found us a house which we have already purchased, thank God! Will you tell the Father Rector this? It is a fine, well situated building adjoining the one we are in. It belonged to a gentleman named Diego de Porras. Father Acosta will describe it to you. Will you give him my kind regards and say that his novices are better pleased every day, as we are with them. They and all the sisters beg to be remembered in your Lordship's prayers. But how ill-mannered I am to give you such messages! However, your humility leads you to submit to whatever is done to you.

You should take no notice of the temptation to give up prayer and should thank God for your desire of practicing it. Be assured that your will wishes to pray and loves to be in God's presence. Nature complains at the idea of using self-constraint. When you feel oppressed, you should move occasionally to some place where you can look at the sky and should walk about for a short time. This will not break off your prayer, and human frailty must be humored lest nature succumb. We are seeking God by such means since we take them for His sake, and the soul must be led gently. However, in this as in all else, the Father Rector will know better than I how to advise you.

We are writing to the Father Visitor who is travelling by slow stages, though the important matter is that you should interview him as he will visit your neighborhood.

I am in good health; God grant that you are and that the cure may benefit you greatly. Today is the third of July.

Your Lordship's unworthy servant and subject,
Teresa de Jesus, Carmelite

Reflection

Perseverance: The temptation to give up prayer is one that St. Teresa herself fell prey to, much to her dismay. She knows well that there are many reasons, all of them bad, that pilgrims on the way cease to pray.

In her case, she convinced herself that her desire for prayer was a lack of humility. It seemed obviously presumptuous to dare to approach God in prayer after having sinned. This kind of self-judgment is very dangerous. About this danger she says in her autobiography:

> In this the devil turned his batteries against me, and I suffered so much because I thought it showed but little humility if I persevered in prayer when I was so wicked, that, as I have already said, I gave it up for a year and a half—at least for a year, but I do not remember distinctly the other six months. This could not have been, neither was it, anything else but to throw myself down into hell; there was no need of any devils to drag me thither. O my God, was there ever blindness so great as this? How well Satan prepares his measures for his purpose when he pursues us in this way! The traitor knows that he has already lost that soul which perseveres in prayer, and that every fall which he can bring about helps it, by the goodness of God, to make greater progress in His service. Satan has some interest in this.

Beyond this tormenting lack of trust that masquerades as humility, she also reveals a few more common reasons for abandonment of prayer. The first is the devil's desire to convince us to break this holy commitment. The enemy's work can bring us to question our right to be in the presence of God and cause us to question whether our prayer is having any effect or is just a waste of time. Regardless of the temptation, Teresa is very strong in her admonition against *any* gap in our daily commitment to prayer. She comes to see her own choice not to pray as a decision to throw herself "down into hell."

Her letter also suggests that even our grace-filled but fallen nature is a source of temptation against the practice of prayer. Though divine life is beginning to unfold in us, Teresa knows that as yet unhealed inclinations and broken impetuses often incline us away from prayer. This is because the Holy Spirit is doing something new, unfamiliar, above what is merely natural. Thus, this movement of the Spirit is specifically supernatural. Our broken sense of self-preservation resists this supernatural work of grace. It is not comfortable to be vulnerable to the immensity of God's goodness. Our need for control and security clashes against the Father's desire to draw us into the orbit of His love and holiness. Yet, whether the source of resistance to prayer is merely human frailty or diabolical craftiness, the answer is always the same: persevere, persevere, persevere.

This perseverance is not complex. It is simply an active rejection of any feeling or thought that would lead us to abandon prayer on any given day. This renunciation is spiritual warfare. It sets itself firmly against the wiles of the devil and refuses to allow the rancor of its insecurities and natural impulses to cause it distress. The decision to deny anything that would oppose prayer makes space in one's life for God to heal and make whole, to restore and raise up.

St. Teresa is ever grounded in a practical understanding of human nature and its frailty. What makes us worthy to pray is not our success in surmounting weakness. Instead, it is always right and just to pray because of the surpassing humility of God who never abandons us. She knows He is always waiting to reveal His merciful love in unexpected and new ways. Behind her teaching, one finds the unfathomable love of God as the justification for our effort to persevere.

On this basis and in this letter, she instructs her reader in a very simple tactic: when oppressive thoughts of unworthiness threaten our prayer, get up, walk outside, and look at the stars. When tormented by "would haves" and "could haves" or anything else that might lessen our devotion to prayer, gaze on the wonders He has fashioned. She points to the divine love letter: the beauty of creation.

For contemplatives, the immensity of the heavens and the inexhaustible number of stars are so many divine invitations to forsake "self" and to lift up one's heart to the Lord. The very splendor of even the visible world is a great help when it comes to persevering in prayer, especially when we feel weak or oppressed by our own pettiness. One of her more powerful maxims uttered on perseverance is worth taking to heart: "God withholds Himself from no one who perseveres."

D𝔸Y 12

LXX
Avila, St. Joseph's Convent, November 1574[1]
To Doña Maria de Mendoza, Valladolid
The Saint longs to see her. Praise of Father Pedro Hernandez. Two postulants. Father Domingo Bañez elected Prior of Truxillo.
Jesus be with your Ladyship!

THEY TELL me you are making great progress in the spiritual life: it is no news to me, but I should like to be nearer to you, and were I not what I am, I should delight in talking to you about such matters. The Father Visitor brings me fresh life, for I do not think he will be deceived about me as everyone else is, because God makes him realize how wicked I am—in fact, he detects imperfections in me at every step. It is an immense comfort to me, and I take care to let him know my faults. It is a great relief to be frank with one who stands [before] us in the place of God, and this I shall be, as long as I have to deal with him. . . .

Your Ladyship's unworthy servant and subject,
Teresa de Jesus, Carmelite

Reflection

Humility: St. Teresa here reveals one of the reasons she is rightly canonized a saint: her profound humility. Because her heart is appropriately ordered to God, she exhibits the exact opposite of the typical

1. Teresa of Avila, *Letters*, vol. 1, excerpts.

human instinct to hide sins and seek to elevate or justify ourselves in the sight of others and God. In fact, she finds comfort and "fresh life" in knowing that she has someone to direct her who is clearly aware of her weaknesses. Why is this?

The reason is simple. If we are to be effectively guided by others, they must be allowed to see and properly understand our sinful tendencies. To the degree we seek to hide, minimize, or obfuscate these realities, our spiritual director will be unable or less able to accurately diagnose and help us overcome those defects that hinder our union with God. It is a sinful and self-centered waste of time to occupy precious moments offered by a busy spiritual director if we are not willing to be brutally honest about our failings and needs.

The other important element revealed in this letter is trust. Teresa desperately wants whatever hinders her ascent to union with God to be uncovered and removed. To achieve this end, she must be able to bear her soul to someone who has a realistic view of her spiritual state. She must also be able to trust that her spiritual director will properly handle this information. In this case she indicates that God has given this priest special insight into the true condition of her soul. This would also mean that he has the wisdom to avoid looking at Teresa only in the light of her weaknesses but also in the light of all that the Holy Spirit is doing in and through her.

This kind of transparency is very challenging. We cannot expect to make spiritual progress without a very open relationship with our spiritual director. Said positively, as we prepare for spiritual direction we should be ready to openly and clearly confess our failures in order to receive the guidance we need. We must also be open to the constructive criticism necessary to reveal destructive elements in our souls that we could not have uncovered ourselves.

Those that are humble and reveal their sins will be healed and will grow in union with God. Those that seek to manage other's perceptions of their spiritual state will find themselves doubly bound: first to the sin that they are entangled in, and then to the additional chains of the sins of pride and vanity.

DAY 13

LXXIII
Valladolid, January 6, 1575[1]
To Don Teutonio de Braganza, Salamanca
Postponement of the foundations at Zamora and Torrijos.
Praise of the Valladolid nuns. Project of a foundation at Madrid. Affairs at Salamanca.
JESUS!

I AM not surprised at your imperfections as I find many in myself, although I have had much more spare time here than I have enjoyed for a long while, which has been a great comfort; may our Lord comfort your soul too, as I beg of Him. Amen. You exaggerate your imperfection; I have experienced something of the sort myself as well as of the rest you mention, but my naturally grateful nature and your zeal make me pass for a very different person from what I really am. And yet I am on my guard! . . .

Your Lordship's unworthy servant,
Teresa de Jesus

Reflection

False Humility: Here we have the opposite problem as revealed in the previous letter where St. Teresa rejoices in her spiritual advisors ability to see her faults. Just as the hiding of faults is rooted in pride and vanity, so exaggerating our faults can also be rooted in pride and vanity.

---

1. Teresa of Avila, *Letters*, vol. 1, excerpts.

This is often called "false humility" or a kind of humility expressed to gain some positive reaction from another rather than a disinterested and sincere expression of the true state of our soul.

Though harder to detect than the kind of pride and vanity that hides weaknesses, this kind of pride can be more dangerous because it masks itself in self-deprecation and a kind of openness to criticism. Often those that harbor this defect are self-deceived into believing that they actually are open to criticism or are self-critical. This deception can be very dangerous as it blinds the pilgrim to their deeply rooted need to be seen as humble when humility is actually in short supply, though desperately needed.

At the same time, the Carmelite doctor of prayer is not surprised or upset by imperfections in others, including false humility. As perfect as her love for God and neighbor had become, she expected imperfection and reveals personal familiarity with it. She also does not let those she loves define themselves in terms of failure. Instead, she zeros in on something good God is doing: in this case, she recognizes her friend's zeal for the Lord. If the great mystic of Avila is self-effacing, it is only with an eye to encouraging a friend who is too preoccupied with her own inadequacy. She does not allow her friend to suffer this inadequacy alone. She identifies with the struggle and discloses it as her struggle too.

Many of those who look to us for affirmation exaggerate their imperfections. Whether we are dealing with our own children, a spouse, or a good friend, St. Teresa's thoughtfulness is good to imitate. Correcting failure should be as brief and succinct as possible. Consoling and affirming what is good in a compelling way takes real discretion and charm.

DAY 14

LXXIV
Valladolid, date unknown.[1]
To the Father Master Luis de Granada, Lisbon
St. Teresa expresses her admiration for
his writings and asks for his prayers.
JESUS!
May the grace of the Holy Spirit ever be with your
Reverence!

I AM one of the many people who love your Reverence in the Lord for your most holy and helpful teaching, and who thank His Majesty for having destined you to do such great and universal good to souls. But for the obstacles of my state and sex, I feel sure that I should have spared no pains to obtain an interview with one whose words have brought me such comfort. Apart from this motive, I have always sought out men like yourself, in order to reassure myself against the fears that have beset my soul for years. Although undeserving of such a favor, I was glad when Señor Don Teutonio told me to write to you, which otherwise I should not have dared to do. Relying upon obedience, I trust our Lord that I shall gain by your remembering to pray for me sometimes, which I greatly need, for, imperfect as I am, I stand in the sight of men with no genuine claim to people's good opinion of me.

If only you realized how true this is, it would win me your help and pity, for knowing the world well, you would understand how severe the

---

trial must be to one who has led an extremely wicked life. Worthless as I am, I have often ventured to pray that you may live a very long while. God grant my petition, and that you may ever grow in holiness and love for Him! Amen.

Your Paternity's unworthy servant and subject,
Teresa de Jesus, Carmelite

I believe that Señor Don Teutonio is one of those deceived regarding me. He tells me of his affection for you, in return for which you ought to pay His Lordship a visit. Trust me, it is not undeserved.

Reflection

Good Counsel: St. Teresa here reveals one of the spiritual growth secrets of the saints: the tireless pursuit of good counsel. So many who are beset with the sins of pride lock themselves into the limitations of their own self-perception. They do so to the peril of their souls as they wrestle with sins and doubt but make little progress.

This self-limitation is like trying to see an entire room of answers while peeking through a keyhole. Instead, we should allow others to help us open the door of insight so that we can gain a broader view of the many ways we can, with the help of grace, overcome sin, increase virtue, mitigate confusion, and effectively ascend the mountain of God.

This master of the interior life incessantly sought the insights of others. She habitually compared their teachings with the wisdom of the Church and sometimes received bad counsel. However, it is clear that, on the whole, the good counsel and its good effects in her far exceeded the bad and the negative effects. So it is with those who constantly seek God and thereby open themselves up to the wisdom and work of the Holy Spirit.

Spiritual Reading: Fr. Luis de Granada was a Dominican and author of spiritual writings prized by St. Teresa and many in the Church to this day. She highly recommended his work *The Sinner's Guide* as particularly helpful. Any pilgrim would be wise to pursue his writings and those others that influenced this great saint; among them are St. Peter of Alcantara's work *Finding God through Meditation*[2] and Fr. Francisco de Osuna's work *Third Spiritual Alphabet*.

Sound theology supports and promotes contemplative prayer. Conversely, contemplative prayer without sound theology is always vulnerable to being misunderstood in very dangerous ways. Teresa had firsthand experience of how hurtful poor theology can be in relation to prayer. She understood that sound doctrine opens the mind to the wonders of God's presence and aids the necessary effort to renounce all kinds of rash judgments concerning the inexhaustible immensity of the love of God.

Spiritual reading of solid theological works can unveil mysteries of the soul's relationship with God that might otherwise remain hidden and uncertain. The writings of any good and saintly theologian or spiritual writer impart the necessary wisdom and insight to overcome many obstacles to our ascent. This type of reading can also inflame the soul with faith, as it experiences the work of God in and through the hearts and minds of those who love Him.

Often, the committed pilgrim feels alone on the journey to God. However, without exception, God never leaves us alone. Spiritual reading is one of the ways to mitigate this loneliness as we engage with other hearts aflame and thereby increase the heat of our own heart as we are drawn to God by the power of their knowledge and love for Him.

---

2. Available through Emmaus Road Publishing or www.NavigatingTheInteriorLife.com.

DAY 15

LXXV
Veas, May 11, 1575[1]
To Don Alvaro de Mendoza, Bishop of Avila
The Saint speaks of Father Gracian whose acquaintance she made at Veas and of his ordering her to make a foundation at Seville.
JESUS!
May the grace of the Holy Spirit ever be with your Lordship!

I REALIZE better every day what grace our Lord has shown me in enabling me to understand the blessings of suffering so that I can peacefully endure the want of happiness in earthly things since they pass so quickly. You must know that I was arranging to spend this summer either at Avila or Valladolid when we received a visit from Father Gracian. He is now Provincial of Andalusia by commission of the Nuncio, who appointed him to this office after the Counter-brief. . . . He has such fine qualities and is a man of such mark that I should be glad if he went to pay his respects to you, so that I might be sure I am not mistaken in my opinion of him. He is anxious to do so since I told him how you have always protected the Order. It is a great consolation to me to know that we have so good a religious.

We shall leave for Seville on the Monday of next week. It is fifty leagues off. I do not think that Father Gracian would have forced me to undertake this work, but his mind was so set on it that, unless I con-

---

1. Teresa of Avila, *Letters*, vol. 1. About a quarter of the leaf is missing.

sented, I should feel very scrupulous about being wanting in obedience, as I always strive to obey strictly. It costs me dear, nor am I very desirous of going through this scorching heat to pass the summer in Seville: God grant it may render Him service! The rest matters little. I beg for your Lordship's blessing; do not forget to pray for me.

As they say there are couriers at Seville. I will write to you when I arrive; there are none at Veas which is a very out-of-the-way place. God grant you good health as I and Father Julian de Avila constantly ask for you. He is a great help to me and begs to be remembered to your Lordship. We often think of you and of St. Joseph's convent, and of the rest I shall enjoy there later on. May it all render God service, and may He watch over you much more vigilantly than over me!

Today is the Eve of the Ascension.

Your Lordship's unworthy servant and subject,
Teresa de Jesus.

Glory be to God, I have kept well ever since I came here and am in much better health than usual.

Reflection

Suffering: "The blessings of suffering" unlock, for the one who welcomes them, the power of patient endurance, and this no matter the hardship. Such blessings are not obvious, even for great mystics like Teresa of Avila. In referring to these mysterious blessings, she does not mean that all suffering is good or that God wants us to suffer. On the contrary, she knows that understanding the wisdom of God, in a lived way, takes prayer, time, careful discernment, and loving obedience. Yet the effort is worth it because it leads to invincible peace.

Those who are patiently faithful in their love for the Lord find joy in discovering how the Lord uses even situations they do not understand to impart His blessings. Indeed, through our obedience in the face of suffering, the Lord provides some of His most beautiful and tender graces, and these are often subtly disguised in circumstances that might seem to be insurmountable and unbearable.

True Christian obedience is never a mechanical response to a command imposed from the outside, purely extrinsic to the interior truth of one's own being. Instead, obedience is a deep vulnerability to the Lord's loving presence who whispers in the ear of our heart. What is whispered is always a blessing, and when whispered in hardship, the fruit of patient endurance is born.

Teresa understood that God uses those with spiritual authority in our lives to help us attend to this whisper. There is always a danger of conflating God's whisper with the noise of our own thoughts. In the Church, Christ has given us one another to protect us from this conflation. We learn what to do in order to say yes to the Lord through people He places over us, even when they make mistakes and cause us to face difficult trials.

Any painful difficulty that we face in obedience to God must be distinguished from suffering brought on for lack of obedience. There are, for example, efforts to escape suffering that rob the heart of its dignity and steal away all courage. We see these effects of selfish escapism in the abuse of drugs, alcohol, food, internet pornography, or relationships. Such webs of sin only limit our freedom to love and bind us from receiving vital blessings. In many ways, such misery is far more severe, dismal, and long lasting than the original suffering we refused to accept.

Such abuses of freedom are incredibly difficult to escape even when a pilgrim finally sees the light. The sense of inadequacy, failure, and shame actually work against the effort to turn to God. When faced with such trials, it is good to remember that patient prayer which obediently trusts in Divine Mercy turns even the burden of sin and shame into a discovery of God's blessing.

His grace is enough for us. Ongoing prayerful acceptance of the loving work of the divine surgeon makes possible a renewed commitment to sobriety and self-discipline every day. This is why, in the difficult daily renunciations and other bitter struggles that recovery requires, there are unique and tender blessings awaiting even the worst of addicts.

Those that aggressively pursue spiritual growth quickly learn that each moment of suffering embraced as an offering of love for the Lord is like another stair step toward heaven. How so? When we embrace suffering, we first avoid the sin and consequences entailed with running from it. Second, we find the great grace of a will strengthened against sin. Third, we begin to rise above the circumstances of life and see God at work in and through challenging situations. This brings us to further comfort and strength. Finally, we gain an understanding of how we can actually participate in the redemptive work of Christ through our suffering.

In this letter, Teresa is again very human in her response. She does not deny suffering or minimize the impact on her. Instead, she thanks God for the grace to understand and accept His mysterious presence. She seems convinced that suffering aids our detachment from the world and our union with God. She then turns to face the suffering, clearly stating what it is and then, with a prayer for God's strength, presses forward in obedience.

The power of this kind of disposition cannot be overstated. Teresa is abandoning herself to obeying God (through her superior) with a clear recognition that she cannot, of her own strength, achieve what He is asking of her. God will never deny a soul that so completely trusts itself to Him.

D🙰Y 16

LXXVII
Seville, June 4, 1575[1]
To Someone Living at Avila
Money matters. Kind wishes.
JESUS!
May the grace of the Holy Spirit ever be with you.

It is a great comfort to me in times of necessity to have so good a trustee as yourself. I am in dire need just now, and entreat you to give all that you can of the funds in deposit to Señor Julian de Avila, in order that he may repay the money lent him for the expenses of the journey. This note, signed with my name, will take the place of a receipt.

Will you pray for me as, sinner though I am, I pray for you; will you also ask Señor Master Daza and my good sister Señora Catalina to do the same? I feel very lonely at being so far away from such a friend as you, but such is life: unless I were resolved to bear the cross, it would make me unhappy. May our Lord grant you the rest I wish for you, and make you very holy!

Signed on June 4, 1575, in the Convent of St. Joseph at Seville.

Your unworthy servant,
Teresa de Jesus, Carmelite

---

1. Teresa of Avila, *Letters*, vol. 1, complete letter.

Reflection

Loneliness: Loneliness is a common struggle for those who seek to give their all to God. In chapter seven of the Gospel of Matthew, Jesus reveals that "few" choose the difficult and narrow path to heaven and "many" choose the wide and easy path to hell. Among those who trek the narrow path, many stop once they achieve a state of prayer and virtue that they feel is adequate to assure their entrance to heaven. An even smaller number refuse to slow their striving on the way until they come to full union with God. These valiant souls will not rest until they have given all that they are to God in this life. Because there are so few on this portion of the mountain, this glorious choice comes with a cross: loneliness.

This loneliness is a longing for the ultimate and full embrace of the beloved in the beatific vision. Teresa realizes that there is no real remedy to this kind of suffering in this life because it is, in some way, God's will as she reveals in her autobiography:

> His will is that such a soul should be lonely and pure with a great desire to receive His graces. If we put many hindrances in the way and take no pains whatever to remove them, how can He come to us and how can we have any desire that He should show us His great mercies?[2]

The sting of loneliness can be momentarily softened when we cross paths with other pilgrims who are just as committed to the way. This fellowship can be an oasis to the soul. However, nothing but God will satisfy the soul that longs for God. Teresa's determination shines through again as she yields to this cross and presses on.

This pressing on can also soften the pain of loneliness because Christ Himself will always accompany those who abandon all for Him.

---

2. Teresa of Avila, *The Life of St. Teresa of Jesus*, 5th ed., trans. D. Lewis, ed. B. Zimmerman (London: Thomas Baker, 1916), 63.

DAY 17

LXXXI
Seville, August 12, 1575[1]
To Doña Juana de Ahumada, Alba de Tormes
Arrival of their two brothers at San Lucar.
Death of Jerome de Cepeda and of Don Lorenzo's wife.
Father Gracian nominated Provincial.
JESUS!

HOWEVER, the joys of this life are always accompanied by troubles, lest we should go crazy with joy. You must know that the good Jerome de Cepeda died like a saint at Nombre de Dios. Pedro de Ahumada has arrived with Lorenzo, who they tell me has lost his wife. Yet we must not grieve for that. I know what kind of life she has led: she has practiced prayer for a long time past and, from what I hear, her death was the wonder of all who witnessed it. One of the three boys Lorenzo was to have brought home with Teresita is also dead. Glory be to God, the rest have reached Spain safe and sound. I am writing to them today and sending them some little things. . . .

Your servant,
Teresa de Jesus

Reflection

"**Lest we should go crazy with joy**": This letter was occasioned by a homecoming, and this particular phrase is filled with a deep mixture

---

1. Teresa of Avila, *Letters*, vol. 1, excerpts.

of emotions that one might not guess a saint would suffer. Those who know how much she loved her brother Lorenzo and how concerned she was for him and her brothers in America better understand the hidden intensity of this document. Her excitement over the return of Lorenzo from America after thirty-four years would have been pure elation had it not been tempered by news of the deaths of Lorenzo's wife, one of his children, and their brother Jerome. This letter was occasioned by Lorenzo's visit to his sister with their troubled brother Pedro, both struggling widowers in a homeland that did not welcome their return.

The contemplative life does not shield a heart from anything that is genuinely human: deep joys and difficult sorrows, excitement of seeing one another again and the heart piercing realization of loss, the tenderness of family affections, genuine concern for those she loved. Instead, the truly prayerful are all the more vulnerable to the plight of those they love, feeling both sorrow and joy more acutely than those whose hearts are hard for lack of prayer. Faith and hope do not diminish such feelings. Instead, they provide the space and courage to seek out God's blessings in the midst of the storms that often rage in our hearts.

In this letter to Juana de Ahumada, we see some of the first signs of just how much care St. Teresa has for her brother's remaining children. Eight-year-old Teresita will be cared for by Teresa's own nuns. The Saint will actively advise her brother concerning the upbringing and education of his remaining sons, while encouraging him to keep his eye on Pedro.

Prayer roots us in the tender reality of love because God is love. We know from Teresa's writings, especially about experiences she describes as "the sleep of the faculties," that there is a kind of spiritual intoxication to which we are vulnerable when we finally begin to see just how much God has done for us and is doing right now. This sober intoxication of the spirit can be brought on from hidden graces poured out in the heart. It can also be occasioned by beautiful heartfelt occasions shared by friends and family. Yet, if we were always caught up in this kind of ecstasy, we would run the risk of being mindlessly unaware of the plight of our brothers and sisters around us.

Her "lest we should go crazy with joy" seen in this context reminds us that the blessings of God not only raise us on high, but help us to enter into the depths where our neighbor is in greatest need. God uses both wonderful moments and difficult ones to deepen His love in us so that we not only feel it, but live it out to the full.

The great Carmelite mystic knows that following Christ means both intoxicating moments of joy and sobering moments of loss and sadness, including even the death of family and close friends. Most of all, she knows that love is not merely sentimental, especially in the face of death. Instead, it looks for reasons to hope and it is always ready to embrace and live within that hope.

DAY 18

XC
Seville, December 30, 1575[1]
To Mother Mary Baptist, Prioress at Valladolid
The Saint receives the order of reclusion.
Lorenzo de Cepeda returns to Seville.
A page boy for his sons. The foundation at Caravaca.
Troubles at the Incarnation. Difficulties of the reform.
Jesus be with you, my daughter, and grant you as many and as happy years as I ask of Him!

WERE I free to choose I should be with you now, for an order from the Most Reverend (Father General) has been notified to me which bids me [to] select a convent in which to remain enclosed forever, also to make no more foundations as, according to the Council, I must not go out again. I understand very well that this is the result of their annoyance at my having come here, and that they think it will pain me keenly, yet I am so glad of it that I fear it will never come to pass. I should choose your convent for many reasons which cannot be stated in writing, except that I should be near my Father and your Reverence. The Father Visitor has not allowed me to leave Seville, and for the present he has more power than the Most Reverend Father General. I do not know what the result will be. It would be a great relief to me to withdraw from all the tumult of the Reform, but God does not choose to deliver me from such crosses which are extremely painful to me. Our Father says that I am to go in the summer. As for this convent—I mean as regards

---

1. Teresa of Avila, *Letters*, vol. 1, excerpts.

its foundation—it has no need of my presence. This place certainly suits my health better, and in a certain sense I am more at peace, as people here do not flatter my vanity as they do in Castile, yet for other reasons it seems better that I should be there again; one thing is that I should be nearer the other houses. May God dispose of the matter, for I wish to have no choice in it and shall be contented wherever I may be sent. . . .

Yours,
Teresa de Jesus

Reflection

Detachment: St. Teresa of Avila reveals a radical availability to the Lord in the face of failure. After Christmas, in 1575, Teresa, now in her sixties, writes to her friend and collaborator in the reform, Mother Maria Bautista. In recent weeks the Inquisition has confiscated her first major spiritual work, her *Life*, tarnishing her reputation and robbing many of confidence in the new Carmelite reform. Her advice and counsel to the leadership has become increasingly unheeded. Instead, her superiors have ordered the Saint not to travel and not to be involved with the reform any longer. She is to find a community where she can live out the remainder of her life as a contemplative nun, and nothing more. Her response? "May God dispose of the matter . . . wherever I may be sent."

Her conscious awareness of being "sent" is an apostolic awareness because an apostle is someone sent by God. She finds no contradiction in this self-awareness with her contemplative vocation. For her apostolic mission and contemplative prayer have become coextensive, a living unity realized in her generous obedience to the Lord and her humble yielding to those with pastoral authority over her. This unity of obedience, generosity, and humility means being radically available to the will of God, whatever it may be. And this is a very safe place for any soul to dwell.

Day 18—Detachment

Here is the great secret of an exalted soul. When our life is all about the will of the Lord, we do not need to worry when He allows us to be misunderstood or mistreated. We do not need to be anxious whether we are successful and impressive or whether we are failures and suffer ruined reputations. God's will is above this world and the opinions of others, and God's plan is not thwarted by our inadequacies and weaknesses. Anyone who stands in this divine wisdom with love discovers an unshakable peace. They might be tested, but they cannot be overcome, because they know that nothing can separate them from the love of God. Possessing all they really need and want in the Lord, they are content with wherever the Lord sends them.

DAY 19

From the Appendix of Volume I of
The Letters of Saint Teresa[1]
**St. Teresa's address to the nuns of the Incarnation
on entering the office of Prioress there in October 1571.**

WHEN THE community went into the Chapter room in the morning, they found the Saint sitting at the feet of the statue of our Lady which she had placed in the stall of the Prioress with the keys of the convent in its hands. She then spoke to them as follows:

Señoras, my Mothers and my Sisters, Our Lord has sent me to this house to undertake my office by order of obedience: an office which I never expected to fill and am very far from deserving. The choice has pained me, for not only does it require of me more than I know how to carry out, but it has also deprived you of your right of free election, giving you a Prioress against your will and choice—and such a Prioress that it will be much if she succeeds in learning the many virtues of the least among you. I came solely to serve and comfort you in every way I could, in which I hope the Master will help me greatly, for in all else every one of you could teach and reform me. Therefore, my Señoras, consider what I can do for each of you, for I would most willingly do it, were it to give my very blood and my life for you. I am a daughter of this house and your sister, and I know the state and the needs of all, or of the greater number of you, so there is no reason why you should hold aloof from one who is so wholly yours. You need not fear my rule, for although hitherto I have lived among and governed Discalced nuns, by the mercy of God, I know how others should be ruled. My desire is that we should all serve God peacefully and that we should do the little enjoined by our Rule and Constitutions for the love of that Master to whom we owe so much. I am well aware of our weakness which is great; yet though our deeds should not attain so far, let our desires do so, for the Lord is compassionate and will by degrees cause our deeds to keep pace with our intentions and longings. (Fuente, Vol. III, p. 152.)

Reflection

Leadership: The monastery of her profession in 1537 had fallen into disarray by 1571. It had already been in spiritual decline when St. Teresa left in 1562, and now the poverty at the Incarnation was so severe that it exceeded any of St. Teresa's monasteries. To make matters worse, Teresa was forced on her sisters by the visitor, Dominican Fray Pedro Fernandez. Their response was in keeping with their spiritual state:

There arose at once a cry of distress from the nuns, who regarded themselves as given over to an enemy; some said they would never obey her, and others reviled her.[2]

During this initial outcry, St. Teresa was on her knees before the Blessed Sacrament. She then rose from prayer and engaged the rebellion with grace and peace.

The trouble and disturbance were so great that some of the nuns fainted through the violence of their distress. The Saint went among them and gently touched them: all in a moment recovered their senses and their reason, and offered no further resistance to her.[3]

---

2. St. Teresa of Avila, *The Book of the Foundations of St. Teresa of Jesus*, trans. D. Lewis, ed. B. Zimmerman (London: Thomas Baker, 1913), xxii.
3. Ibid.

Even so, matters worsened before they improved.

> Others, however, still remained obstinate in their rebellion, and bent on disobedience to the last; but the Saint was patient and gentle, and exercised her authority as if she had none; nevertheless she intended to be obeyed, and accordingly on the first chapter day the nuns on entering the choir saw the image of our Lady in the seat of the prioress, and St. Teresa sitting at her feet. The rebellious nuns were struck by a heavenly terror, and changed their minds: all signs and all desires of disobedience vanished, and the Saint was obeyed as prioress with as much readiness and affection as if she had been chosen by them of their own free will.[4]

There are many leadership principals that could be gleaned from St. Teresa's life and this case of dramatic success in the face of aggressively irrational opposition. This event is worthy of much reflection by any in a position of authority.

For our purposes, we will focus on two simple elements: prayer and humility. As Teresa was announced to the monastery, she was in prayer. She knew what she was up against, as after her first departure, there was a great cry of outrage against her. She had rejected their diseased and lukewarm expression of Carmelite spirituality and they were wounded. Beyond this troublesome history, she caught wind of the resistance before she arrived. But, rather than standing tall and firm before all and taking control of the situation as any strong leader might, she humbly dropped to her knees before the Lord.

When she arose, she did so by the gentle strength and grace of God. The fruits of this reality can be clearly seen by the dramatic changes in those around her. She so powerfully demonstrated the love and gentleness of God that the hardest of hearts were softened and:

> From that day forth the nuns of the Incarnation gave no trouble to the prioress, and the abuses of the house were all corrected; though

---

4. Ibid.

under the mitigated observance, which was never changed, the nuns lived as if they were under the reform of St. Teresa; their temporal and spiritual necessities, hitherto so great and serious, were at once supplied; and the seed of good, sown in such good soil, grew and bore fruit so abundantly that the monastery of the Incarnation became from that day forth one of the pearls of the old observance.[5]

The exercise of power and dominance is an easy path taken by most in authority. This approach rarely, if ever, wins the hearts and minds of its subordinates; and those that follow are often muted and less full of life; their minds and hearts unable to fully commit to the mission forced upon them.

In contrast, the slower more patient way of love, even a firm love that is clear and unwavering in its means and ends, allows God to bring about the conversion of hearts; truly converted hearts are a powerful force for good that can never be gained by force.

5. Ibid.

DAY 20

CXLIII
Toledo, November 26, 1576[1]
To Don Luis de Cepeda, At Torrijos
Acknowledgment of money received.
Sister Beatriz of Malagon. Spiritual advice.
JESUS!
May the grace of the Holy Ghost
be ever with your Honor.

I RECEIVED your letters and the four ducats; the sum will be paid this week. May our Lord reward you for your care of our sister of the Incarnation, for she is in the greatest need of all. Sister Beatriz is now in charge of the convent at Malagon on account of the illness of the Mother Prioress. She manages it exceedingly well, thank God! I did not think she was capable of it.

You must not be surprised at being unable to be very recollected in the midst of all your worries: it would be an impossibility. I shall be quite satisfied if you return to your good rule of life when you are freed from them. God grant that you may follow it faithfully. Do not be much concerned as to whether your fortune is large or small, for even if it is very large, all will soon come to an end.

I ask the prayers of these ladies, and the Mother Prioress begs for yours.

---

1. Teresa of Avila, *The Letters of Saint Teresa*, trans. Benedictines of Stanbrook (London: Thomas Baker, 1921), vol. 2, complete letter. Hereafter: *Letters*, vol. 2.

Today is November 26.

Your unworthy servant,

Teresa de Jesus

Reflection

Prayer in the Midst of Worry: The great doctor of prayer has much wisdom to offer regarding the practice of recollection. She knows that this simple effort to focus one's attention on God is very beneficial and, under normal conditions, highly recommends the practice. She is obviously more concerned about the practice of this kind of mental prayer than she is about Don Luis Cepeda's finances.

Always a realist who understands that we need to adapt our devotional practices as we confront life's challenges, she approaches her cousin's concerns about prayer with common sense. There are circumstances when it is impossible to be recollected, but even in the face of such challenges, it is possible to live a prayerful life. It is a matter of following and adapting the program of prayer and devotion to which one has committed oneself. This is what she means by "rule of life," which is nothing else than a plan for loving God.

Teresa is not surprised that her cousin Luis is struggling to draw his heart past his worries to the heart of God. As the brother of Sister Beatriz, about whom she reports and two other sisters who are also Carmelites, St. Teresa knows she is addressing someone who is from an entire family dedicated to mental prayer.

He is himself obviously so accustomed to being recollected that it disturbs him, in the midst of his current anxieties, not to be constantly aware of the Lord's presence. If he were not already a prayerful man, then his inability to recollect himself would not have caused him stress. He is, however, stressed and anxious that he has to struggle to rest his heart in the Lord's presence. On this point, Teresa reassures him that under his present circumstances, maintaining a recollected state of mind would be impossible.

Rule of Life: Stewing over our experience (or lack thereof) in prayer becomes an excessive preoccupation when it distracts us from the love we owe God and those He entrusts to us. A self-centered approach to monitoring our spiritual state rarely if ever brings deeper peace and strength to the soul. This is why St. Teresa directs her cousin away from worrying about what is "impossible" and centers him on what can be done: his rule of life.

It is noteworthy that St. Teresa does not burden Don de Cepeda with new techniques and practices in prayer. Her goal is not to help him re-achieve the state of recollection to which he had been accustomed. This spiritual accomplishment is not the way forward for him as he deals with the business affairs entrusted to him as a layman in the world. Instead, she directs his attention to the rule of life to which he is already committed. She wants him to discover how faithfulness to spiritual discipline, rather than success in spiritual accomplishments, is the pathway to holiness.

Holiness subordinates material concerns to what is spiritual. Holiness also subordinates spiritual accomplishments and achievements to faithfulness. Faithfulness in the life of prayer is not about achieving states of consciousness or degrees of prayer. True faithfulness in our devotion to the Lord is about the observance of simple practices done with reverent humility and great love. Love alone maintains a discipline of life commensurate with the responsibilities that the Lord has entrusted to us.

Teresa's counsel helps us to see that a personal plan of love or rule of life is a profound and useful secret for spiritual growth. Not only priests and religious but anyone who desires holiness can discern and develop this tool with the help of a good spiritual director.[2] It is simply a clear

---

2. Dan Burke outlines an effective approach to this practice in his book, *Navigating the Interior Life: Spiritual Direction and the Journey to God* available at Emmaus Road Publishing.

and specific daily plan regarding how we will express our love to God. It can be as simple as:

6:00 a.m.: Rise and make a Morning Offering. For example, make the Sign of the Cross, take a moment to thank God for a new day, pray Morning Prayer or a decade of the Rosary, or slowly recite a psalm; spend a few minutes in silent mental prayer, spiritual reading or Bible reading, and end by asking God for help in being faithful in your service to your family and to those with whom you work.

9:00 a.m.: Take two minutes to be mindful of the presence of God.

11:30 a.m.: Go to Mass.

3:00 p.m.: Take five minutes to remember the Passion of the Lord or pray the Chaplet of Divine Mercy.

7:00 p.m.: Pray a family Rosary (even if just an Our Father, Hail Mary and Glory Be with young children), Evening Prayer, or slowly pray the Magnificat.

9:00 p.m.: Examine your conscience and ask yourself how well you followed your plan of love (rule of life), make an act of contrition and entrust yourself to the Lord's mercy, pray night prayer, or slowly pray a psalm before retiring for the evening.

The key is to establish a daily spiritual rhythm that works with the circumstances and obligations that are part of daily life. This plan develops and becomes more useful as it is carefully refined and adapted with the counsel of a good spiritual director or confessor over time. When prudently applied, this schedule of spiritual practices becomes a powerful remedy to all kinds of spiritual anxieties which we should not waste time fretting over.

DAY 21

CXXVI
Toledo, October 1576[1]
To Father Gracian, Seville
Father Gracian and the Calced friars.
Paul and Joseph. Counsels on prayer.
JESUS!
May the grace of the Holy Ghost be with your Paternity,
my Father.

I RECEIVED three letters from you today by the head courier, and others brought by Fray Alonso yesterday. God has well repaid me for the delay. May He be forever praised for your Reverence's good health.

It was a great shock to me, on examining the two parcels from the Mother Prioress, to find no letter from you: you can imagine what I felt. But things were soon put right. Will you always let me know which of my letters you receive, for you often write without answering my questions and also forget to give the date. In your last two letters you asked me how I liked Doña Juana although I had already told you in the letter sent by the courier of Toledo. As I expect your reply will arrive in those you tell me are coming by way of Madrid, I suppose that there is not much amiss.

I am well and my Isabel furnishes us with recreation: her content and happiness are wonderful. I wrote to Doña Juana yesterday. All are well.

---

1. Teresa of Avila, *Letters*, vol. 2, complete letter.

I have thanked God from my heart for the way in which our affairs are progressing. I was astonished at what Fray Alonso tells me is being said about your Paternity. God bless me! How necessary your journey was! Had you done nothing else I think you were bound in conscience to do this for the honor of the Order. I do not know how they could publish such calumnies: may God enlighten these fathers. Had your Paternity someone whom you could trust, it would be a very good plan to give them another prior, but since there is no one else, I was astonished at hearing who made that suggestion, which would have no result. It would be a great thing to have someone there who was not opposed to us in every way, if you thought well of the idea. Great difficulties might arise if the present prior should refuse to resign. These fathers do not appear to wish to be slighted, which is not surprising.

I am more surprised at Paul, busy as he is, being able to fulfill his obligations towards Joseph so peacefully: I thank God sincerely for it. Will your Paternity tell Paul to be satisfied at last with his prayer and not to be concerned about using his intellect when God grants him a favor of another kind; say that I am much pleased with what he wrote to me. As regards the interior things of the spirit, the most acceptable and effectual prayer is that which produces the best results. By this I do not mean a number of desires at a time which, although good, are not always what our self-love paints them, but effects manifested by deeds and desires for the glory of God shown by the soul's seeking it sincerely, so that the memory and understanding are employed in pleasing Him and in proving our love for Him to the uttermost.

Oh, what genuine prayer this is! But not so a sweetness which ends in our own enjoyment. When prayer is accompanied with such sweetness, it leaves the soul feeble and timid and very sensitive to human respect. I wish for no prayer that does not make me grow in virtue. If it were accompanied by violent temptations, aridities, and trouble, and left me more humble, I should consider it a good prayer, for the more it pleases God, the better the prayer in my opinion.

May He deign to preserve your Paternity for us as I desire,
Teresa de Jesus

Reflection

Reverent Discretion Concerning Spiritual Things: The "Paul" to
whom St. Teresa is offering a word of consolation regarding progress in
prayer is her canonical superior in the reform, Fr. Gracian. We see in
other letters that she uses code names to protect the privileged content
from being abused by anyone who might intercept her message. When
it comes to the intimate details of another's spiritual life, every Christian has the responsibility to observe careful discretion so that sensitive details do not become a matter of gossip or character assassination.
Spiritual matters of this most intimate kind should be treated with great
reverence and sensitivity.

Transition to Contemplation: Teresa counsels Fr. Gracian "not to
be concerned about using his intellect when God grants him a favor of
another kind." Teresa knows that Fr. Gracian is beginning to emerge
beyond discursive meditation to a deeper kind of prayer. She knows this
because the letter indicates that Fr. Gracian has struggled with how to
respond to mystical graces he is receiving in prayer. She wants to address
his anxiety over whether he is properly participating in prayer if he is not
using his intellect during prayer. We know from *The Interior Castle* (particularly in chapter four) that Teresa counsels against utilizing methods
to suppress thoughts or the imagination during prayer. She forcefully
argues against all deliberate efforts to empty the mind in prayer.

Teresa teaches that when one begins to be called by God beyond
meditation, the Blessed Trinity will engage the mind in such a manner
that its natural operation can be momentarily suspended or elevated.
The Holy Spirit performs a supernatural work that lifts the mind and
soul where no natural effort could ever take it. The Word of the Father

touches the mind, completely captivating it and bathing it in such wonder that it is difficult to think or finish a meditation.

Sometimes these moments of wonder and ecstasy continue even while the soul does not realize what has happened to it. It can also be the case that the soul feels a certain frustration during this disruptive but transformative change in prayer. It is common that the soul feels it might be unproductive and wasting its time because the soul does not recognize that these sparks of mystical prayer are a transitional call into even deeper encounters with the Lord. Because this new and unfamiliar kind of prayer is such a great work in the soul, those that experience it need to patiently yield to the Holy Spirit and try not to force themselves back into a discursive mode of prayer.

Discerning Authentic Contemplative Prayer: The great mystic of Avila then explains how to determine whether "favors" or what seem to be contemplative graces are authentic.

It is clear from St. Teresa's inference that these kinds of experiences can emanate either from our imagination or from the deception of the enemy. Souls that are addicted to sweetness and satisfaction in prayer are vulnerable to grave deceptions. Her wisdom offers a more reliable standard for discernment.

The central question when discerning whether or not "sweetness" in prayer is from God concerns what St. Teresa calls "the results." The fruit that remains afterward is the primary determining factor, not the consolation itself.

Do these experiences inflame the heart to self-giving to God and others or do they produce pride and confusion? Any breaking forth of affections that bind us more deeply in service to Christ and His Mystical Body following from prayer, even when the intellect feels unproductive and reason remains unsatisfied, can only come from the Spirit of Love Himself.

In contrast, false mystical graces will leave the soul self-centered, lacking in peace (usually after an initial good feeling), and generally disposed to self-interest with a focus on the experience rather than self-forgetfulness and self-giving.

DAY 22

CXXVII
Toledo, October 23, 1576[1]
To Father Gracian, Seville
True prayer. Laurencia detects the devil's plots.
Prayer of Sisters San Jeronimo and Beatriz.
Father Gracian's sermons.

Do NOT suppose that one who suffers does not pray; he prays, since he offers his sufferings to God, and often far better than one who is racking his brains in solitude and who fancies, if he manages to wring out a few tears, that this is true prayer.

Will your Paternity forgive this long message to Paul; you will bear with it because of your affection for him. If you think I am right, repeat it to him; if not, say nothing about it. I have stated what I wish for myself: I assure you that good works and a clear conscience are great things. . . .

I was very envious of the nuns who heard your Paternity's sermons. Evidently they deserved that, and I deserve crosses; may God give me more to bear for love of Him. . . .

God give you the rest I desire for you and the sanctity He can bestow. Amen.

Today is October 23.

---

1. Teresa of Avila, *Letters*, vol. 2, excerpts.

Your Paternity's unworthy servant,
Teresa de Jesus

Reflection

Suppositions About Suffering: "Do not suppose that one who suffers does not pray." Jesus was once confronted with a similar charge in the Gospel of St. John (chapter nine) when He was asked, "Rabbi, who sinned, this man or his parents, that he was born blind?" Jesus answered, "It was not that this man sinned, or his parents, but that the works of God might be made manifest in him" (Jn 9:2–3).

Here, Teresa, the wise mystic, similarly addresses the concern that someone who suffers must be in sin or not really praying, which leads us to question our own suppositions about the life of prayer. In our time, the "prosperity gospel" proposes that if we have faith, our life will be one that is absent of undesirable circumstances. Another subtle form of this error is the assumption that when we pray, there should always be some form of tangible consolation or tangible good that emerges from it.

Sometimes those who promote these ideas unintentionally discourage others who struggle to pray. When suffering is great, it can at times feel impossible to pray. Sometimes all that can be managed is a broken effort to make the Sign of the Cross, a few fragmented syllables of a Hail Mary, or simply a sense of yearning for God hidden in the difficult silence of physical or psychological agony.

Regardless, though physical and other suffering can come due to sin, one should never jump to conclusions about the spiritual state of a soul when they are suffering.

Suffering and Spirituality: Is there a redemptive meaning to suffering when one's own efforts to pray seem futile and meaningless? Can the crushing alienation that suffering itself brings become a prayer? The clarity of Christ regarding the man born blind shines through St. Teresa in her brief "Do not suppose. . ."

No, suffering does not prevent mental prayer. In fact, those who suffer have the gates of true prayer opened to them in ways that even those performing retreat exercises do not enjoy. The prayer offered when one is too weak to conjure the right emotions, too feeble even to be aware that one prays at all, is all the more perfect and acceptable to God.

True Prayer, Better Prayer: True prayer is not about the noisy efforts of our own reason, conjuring an awareness of experiences, or producing psychic states, nor even the very noble and necessary state of contrition. There is a deeper kind of repentance and a better kind of prayer that the Carmelite doctor proposes to us.

Sorrow over sin is never a bad thing, but she wants us to understand that aptitude in performing mental gymnastics does not achieve better prayer. For her, true prayer is a simple movement of the heart to God, a humble surrender of oneself into His hands, an offering in the hidden silence of love.

True prayer lives within a simple act of the will, a decision to love God and neighbor, even when one is completely powerless to act, think or be aware of one's own experience. Saint Teresa's succinct "Do not suppose" reminds us that the more rooted in reality and the more rooted in love we are, the better our prayer will be. On every practical and visible level, such a decision to love may remain completely hidden in the physical and mental misery of the moment. Yet this silent decision, this spiritual offering, remains true prayer, a better contemplation.

Prayer is effectual when it is rooted in devotion and reality, sacrifice and relationship, love and truth. God is drawn by our loving reverence, not our emotional states; our poverty, not our mental feats; our lowliness, not our spiritual thrones. This is vital to remember when we go on retreat or attempt spiritual exercises. It is also a vital truth to return to when we find ourselves a little too preoccupied with the psychological movements we expect in meditation. It is a word of hope for those who suffer. "Do not suppose" that prayer is ever about successfully attaining the consolation we think we deserve; instead, prayer is always better when it learns to rely on the Lord in the silence of love.

DAY 23

CXXX
Toledo, November 2, 1576[1]
To Mother Mary Baptist, Prioress Of Valladolid
**Health of the prioress. Matters of the Order and
the convent of Valladolid.**
JESUS!
May the grace of the Holy Spirit be with you.

TAKE NO notice of the interior troubles you mention; the greater they are, the more you ought to despise them. They arise from a strong imagination and a disordered body, and the devil, seeing this, contributes his share. But do not be frightened, for "God will not suffer you to be tempted above that which you are able," and though you may fancy that you consent, you do not, but are acquiring merit. For the love of God get well, eat enough, and do not be alone or think much. Occupy yourself with what you can and how you can. . . .

Let me know soon how you are, and abide with God. The Mother Prioress was grieved at hearing of your illness. All here are praying for you. Always send my kind regards to Fray Domingo when you write to him, and tell me about his health.

Today is All Souls' Day.

Yours,

Teresa de Jesus

---

1. Teresa of Avila, *Letters*, vol. 2, excerpts.

Reflection

Internal and External Trials and Spiritual Warfare: The prioress of Valladolid has obviously revealed a number of personal struggles to Teresa, and Teresa responds with clarity but also with gentle care. Her advice is very simple and straight forward, yet also insightful regarding the work of the enemy.

She knows of the prioress' strong powers of imagination and notes that her internal discord is coming in part from a kind of preoccupation or focus on thoughts, worries, or whatever is troubling her. It seems that her physical health also makes these troubles even worse. Here, Teresa makes an interesting comment about the devil's work.

Some see the enemy as the cause of all that ails us or makes us uncomfortable. This is obviously not a view that can stand the test of Scripture or tradition. Even so, the enemy is always looking for an opportunity to tempt us. As an opportunistic thief is ever searching for a way to steal the goods of another, so the enemy is always looking for circumstances that are favorable to his destructive work on the soul. In this case, he knows that the prioress' mind is a bit overactive and that she doesn't feel well physically. Teresa reveals that such conditions are commonly present when the enemy enters, to seek to make matters worse and to use circumstances as an opportunity to draw the soul into confusion and desolation. Teresa's wise remedies are almost universally applicable:

Find peace in the loving arms of God, knowing that He will give you the grace you need to endure the suffering you face. A good Carmelite would know to both affirm this truth as an act of faith and dwell on this truth so as to make it a lived experience.

Take care of your body. The life of a Carmelite nun during this period was very austere and difficult and involved fasts and penitential practices that were hard on the body. Teresa gives her permission to the prioress, as she often did with others, to rest and care for herself.

Get busy, spend time with others, serving others. The life of a Carmelite was also one of solitude for the purpose of prayer. However, in times of temptation and difficulty, we often need to engage and serve others in order to break our minds out of the prison of dwelling on our own struggles.

DAY 24

CXLV
Toledo, about November 1576[1]
To Father Gracian, Seville
Calumnies. A case of diabolical possession. Father
Gracian's sleep.

. . . ALTHOUGH DEEPLY grieved at such infamies being uttered against your Paternity, I greatly admire the prudence with which you have acted; I assure you that God loves you dearly, my Father, and that you imitate Him faithfully. Rejoice, for He sends you the crosses you ask for and He will defend you, for He is just: may He be forever blessed!

As for the affair of this girl or woman, I feel thoroughly convinced that she is not influenced so much by melancholia as by the devil, who has entered into her to invent these falsehoods. It is he and nothing else; and after having deceived her, he is trying to entrap you in some way. Therefore you must act with extreme caution and must by no means visit her house lest you should meet with the fate of St. Marina—I think her name was—who was accused of being the mother of some child and suffered much from the calumny. This is not the time for you to meet such a trial. In my poor opinion, you ought to withdraw from the matter; there are others who can look to this soul, while your Paternity has many souls to benefit by your care. Take notice, my Father, that unless this woman gave you the letter under the seal of confession, or during

1. Teresa of Avila, *Letters*, vol. 2. The beginning and the end are lost.

her confession, it is a case for the Inquisition, and the devil lays many snares. A person was condemned to death by the Inquisition for the very same thing, I am told. Not that I believe the woman of whom you speak gave the letter to the demon, for he would not have returned it so quickly. She must be telling some falsehood (God forgive me for saying so) and must like talking to your Reverence. Perhaps the whole tale is her invention, but I should like to see your Paternity far away from the place so as to cut the matter short more effectually.

But how malicious I am! There is need to be in this life. On no account dream of setting things right in four months. It is a very risky affair; others may see to it. If any denunciation is to be made against this woman in matters outside the confessional, you are warned beforehand, for I fear the affair may be made public and you may be severely blamed for having known of it and kept silence. But I see that it is foolish of me to insist, as your Paternity already knows that. . . .

I thank our Lord sincerely for having given you such peace and a desire to please Him in all things. The light He grants you from time to time concerning spiritual joys is a special mercy shown you. His Majesty succors us in proportion to our trials, and yours being great, so are His favors. May His Name be praised forever.

I assure you, my Father, that it would be well for you to take sufficient rest. Being extremely hard worked, you would not feel the fatigue until your head was too exhausted to recover, and you know how important your health is to us. For the love of God, take other people's advice in this case; put aside your business, however pressing, and even your prayer when it is time for you to sleep. Be sure you grant me this request, for when the devil sees spiritual fervor, he often represents things as being very important for God's service so as to stop in one way the good he could not hinder otherwise. . . .

Reflection

Trials and Our Needs: There are three spiritual gems in this letter. The first concerns the "light" of the Lord's favor in the face of trials. The second addresses the necessity of tending to our earthly needs. The third is a vital observation that should inform our discernment of God's will. What she has carefully set together for Father Gracian is a beautiful piece of spiritual jewelry for our life of prayer.

When considering the "light" God gives when we face difficult challenges, St. Teresa observes that the Lord "succors us in proportion to our trials." We can take this in two ways. We can look at this statement in terms of the delight that comes from being spiritually fruitful. We can also consider this "proportion" in terms of our awareness of God's presence. The divine light Teresa proposes in times of trials can allow us to delight in either the exquisite work God is accomplishing or in His presence itself or both.

This "light" of "proportion" to which St. Teresa appeals proposes the particular way in which God reveals Himself as the One who delights in us. The Saint presumes that we know how unity with the Trinity makes us fully alive. The Carmelite reformer hopes we already have experienced God delighting us in the midst of all kinds of endurance, hardship, sacrifice, renunciation: in a word, through the Cross.

The Lord delights in a soul commensurate to its hardships because the Almighty Father is not limited by what is easiest and most comfortable. He does not confine Himself to the most powerful or successful. Within the limits of human frailties and needs, lowliness and simplicity, humility and reverence, this doctor of the Church wants us to discover the tenderness by which God magnifies His limitless glory. It is this desire of God not to surmount the limits of our nature, but to work within them, that leads us to a consideration of the *necessity of tending to our earthly needs* or as Teresa counsels, the need that we have to take "sufficient rest."

An excessive zeal in our service to the Lord can be just as dangerous as a lack of zeal. Most people, in fact, struggle to have any zeal at all, and the purpose in most of her writing is to address this deficiency. But in this letter to her spiritual leader, she has discerned that he is running himself ragged and not accepting the poverty of his own humanity.

God's will is accomplished not by surmounting the limits of our humanity through superhuman feats and achievements. God is not served when we exhaust ourselves to the breaking point by keeping a hectic pace of life. It is an expression of non-Christian utilitarianism to believe that greater progress is accomplished by greater effort. Under such a limited spirit, we can be easily self-deceived, and under this deception, self-destruction follows.

"When the devil sees spiritual fervor, he often represents things as being very important for God's service so as to stop in one way the good he could not hinder otherwise."

Discernment of Spirits: In his Rules of Discernment of Spirits, St. Ignatius bases his counsels on this observation as well. Both St. Ignatius and St. Teresa (who benefitted from the counsel of some truly great Jesuit spiritual directors) recognize the spiritual battle faced by fervent souls dedicated to doing something beautiful for God. The same forces that oppose God also oppose what is authentically human. Those who are fervent are rarely seduced into outright evil actions. But they can often be deceived and confused when lesser goods are presented as the greater good. This is why the wisdom of discernment becomes increasingly important in the Christian life.

Pope Francis once told a reporter that the wisdom of discernment redeems the necessary ambiguities of life by helping us find the most appropriate means to serve the Lord. Why are there ambiguities and why does the Lord allow fervent souls to struggle with deceptive and confusing spirits? There is much to say on this point, but for our purposes here it is enough to remember that the Lord tests us as a necessary means to bring His work to perfection in us. In this divine work, even evil spirits are subject to Him. Sometimes God mysteriously allows the malice of these spirits to produce something beautiful in the freedom of the soul, to help the soul in its own liberty to enter more deeply in the mystery of obedience, the same obedience that Christ rendered the Father.

Teresa wants Fr. Gracian, the priest whom God has chosen to lead the reform, to proceed not as someone driven by the challenges and difficulties that any authentic effort to renew the spiritual life entails. Fr. Gracian need not lose sleep calculating the best solutions to the problems he confronts. Nor should he neglect getting the rest he needs, even when it comes to something as important as his spiritual exercises. St. Teresa wants Father Gracian and each of us to take the time we need for careful discernment regarding the most appropriate means of serving the Lord.

To accomplish a spiritual work, one must go by a spiritual means, even if it seems inefficient and more vulnerable. We need to trust that the Lord will sustain us with the spiritual delight and refreshment we need when the time arises. In our service, we need to prudently take care of not only our spiritual needs but our physical needs as well. Finally, we must bring the wisdom of discernment into the spiritual battle into which we have been sent. It is a matter of total obedience and surrender to the Divine Will, even when this surrender involves something as simple and earthly as sleep.

DAY 25

CXLVI
Toledo, about November 1576[1]
To Father Gracian, Seville
Father Gracian's enemies. His need of sleep.

I SENT a letter last week by the courier of Toledo in answer to what Paul says about the tongues. When I was speaking to Joseph, he told me to warn Paul that he has many enemies, visible and invisible, and must guard against them. That is why I do not wish him to trust so implicitly in the "Egyptians" or the "owls."

. . . On reading Paul's letter again, I find that he says that he sacrifices his sleep to "think things over," and I believe he means on account of transports of prayer. He ought not to accustom himself to neglect so great a treasure except for the sleep that his body requires, for God bestows most precious gifts at such times and I am not astonished at the devil's trying to deprive Paul of them. As this favor cannot be enjoyed at will, we must prize it when God bestows it. His Majesty then gives us more light as to how to serve Him than our intellect could obtain if it forsook the favor it is enjoying, to search on its own account. But believe me, I have spoken the truth: follow my advice about sleep unless you have business of such importance on hand that it would keep you awake; but if sleep comes, there will be time enough afterwards to think about your work.

---

1. Teresa of Avila, *Letters*, vol. 2, fragment of a letter.

I read in some book that if we leave God when He seeks us, when we seek Him, we shall not find Him.

Reflection

Human Frailty and Limitations: We have already commented on why "sufficient rest" is important for the spiritual life. What happens, however, when there are special graces of prayer, graces so intense that we seem transported beyond the limits of space and time? The Carmelite doctor calls these graces "transports of prayer," spiritual treasures which ought not be neglected except "for the sleep that the body requires."

The adversary tempts the fervent to neglect their personal needs, suggesting that union with God was not something achieved through our frail humanity but despite it. He suggests to fervent souls that the way forward is to surmount our natural limits, as if God were not aware of these when He gave us the gift of His sanctifying presence. The evil one wants us to rely on our own spiritual achievements and to be distracted by experiences in prayer. He knows that when we seek such experiences, we are distracted from the divine intimacy that we otherwise might know. God, however, is not thwarted by this diabolical effort. He presides over all and uses even Satanic deception to purify and intensify our friendship with Him. This is why He mysteriously permits the adversary to test us, even to the point of mimicking sublime favors. For our part, it is the safer route not to rely on what we can achieve or what we feel in prayer, no matter how sublime the experience. Instead, we overcome every spirit who might stand in our way through humble faith animated by patient love. On this point the great Carmelite mystic is inviting us to share with her a deep spiritual truth. Living faith knows that sleep as well as wholesome forms of recreation are not in themselves opposed to the glory of God. Such faith also knows that there are blessings greater than even what would seem to be the sublimity of mystical experience. The Lord is prepared to give such blessings when we address our physical limitations as creatures. It is the first degree of love for God to show our gratitude to Him by patiently addressing our bodily needs, including the need for proper rest. Teresa of Avila is confident that the Lord pours out gifts on those He loves even as they slumber (cf. Ps 127:2).

Is there a theological justification for St. Teresa's insistence that Fr. Gracian should attend to his need for proper rest even before his desire for spiritual experiences in prayer? By becoming flesh, the Word of the Father reveals to us how the Holy Spirit prefers to work within the limits of human nature to manifest the limitlessness of God's nature. Thus, not only did the Lord work wonders and preach and pray through the night, He also ate and slept. And in all that He accomplished, He acted with all His soul and might for the glory of the Father.

Against this theological reality of Christ's own example we can understand St. Teresa's admonition to put rest before pursuit of mystical experience. Once we have set our hearts on serving the Lord, we must humbly recognize our limitations and renounce allowing ourselves to be driven by any spirit other than the Holy Spirit, who does not drive but draws. He loves us in our humanity, and wants nothing more than for us to thrive—to live life to the full in and through this humanity animated by His love.

The Father pours out His blessings whether we are asleep or awake as long as we are faithful to the responsibilities entrusted to us. Any other spirit (arising from one's own psychology or outside it) that opposes this Divine Munificence deceives, thwarts, and oppresses. These spirits promise lesser goods so that we will neglect the greater blessing the Father yearns to give. When such a spirit provides a transporting experience that seems to lift us above time and space, it is not given to help us thrive, but only to deprive us of the Father's blessing of a good night's sleep.

DAY 26

CLXVI
Toledo, January 17, 1577[1]
To Don Lorenzo de Cepeda
Advice about prayer. Present of a hair shirt. Father
Gracian visits the communities.
Jesus be with your Honor.

I TOLD you in the letter sent by the Alba courier that the sardines were fresh when they arrived and that the sweets came in good time, but I wish you had eaten them yourself. May God repay you. Do not send me anything more; I will ask for it when I require anything. You are most welcome to live in our quarter of the town, but examine the room of which I spoke carefully. Unless repaired it would be dangerous, for it needed looking to. See to that and to the rest of the house.

As for secrecy about my affair, I do not say that it is binding under pain of sin. I am very averse to such agreements, for you might forget; it is enough for you to know that it would pain me if you talked about it. My confessor had already told me that your vow was invalid, which is a great relief to me as I felt exceedingly anxious about it. I also consulted him about the vow of obedience to me, which seemed out of place. He approves of it as long as you make no promise either to me or anyone else. Therefore I wish you to make no pledge about it; and even then I dislike it. However, as it is a comfort to you, I submit on the condition that you take no vow of obedience to anybody. I am glad you see that

1. Teresa of Avila, *Letters*, vol. 2, excerpts.

Fray Juan understands your case: he has experienced it as even Francisco has, although not to the same extent as God has granted you. May He be forever praised to all eternity. He favors both of us now.

What kindness our Lord shows us! He seems to wish to prove His greatness by upraising us wretched creatures with such sublime favors, for I know of no one viler than you and I. For more than a week I have been in a spiritual state which, if it continues, may cause me ill success with my many business affairs. Before I last wrote, my ecstasies had returned, which distressed me as they sometimes occurred in public and during Matins. Resistance is useless and they cannot be concealed. I felt so utterly ashamed that I wanted to hide myself no matter where. I have prayed earnestly that I may no longer have raptures in public; will you pray about it, for there are many disadvantages and it does not seem to me a higher form of prayer.

During the last few days I have appeared to be half intoxicated: at least it is evident that the soul is well off, but the powers being bound, it finds it difficult to attend to anything except Him Whom it loves. During the preceding week I was often incapable of a single good thought, being in a state of complete aridity. In fact, in one way I was rather glad of it, as I had been in my present state for several days and it is a joy to realize how little we can do ourselves. Blessed be He Who can do all things! Amen. I have told you much: the rest cannot be written or even spoken about. We two ought to thank our Lord on each other's account: at least you should do so for me, as I am unable to thank Him as I ought and need much help from others.

I do not know what to say to you about the favor of which you tell me, which is certainly higher than you realize and will be the beginning of great good unless you forfeit it through your own fault.

I have passed through this state of prayer after which, as a rule, the soul enjoys peace and sometimes wishes to perform penance, especially if the impulse of love has been very strong. The soul then seems as though it could not endure doing nothing for God, for this is a touch which transforms the soul into love, and if it increases you will understand what was mysterious to you in the verses, for it is keen pain and sorrow, yet most delicious, coming from we know not whence. In fact, the love of God wounds the soul which cannot tell where the wound comes from, nor how it came, nor whether it is wounded, or what is taking place, yet feels a delicious anguish which makes it complain, so that it cries:

> . . . Thou dost deign
> Without a wound our hearts to pain
> Without a pang, our wills to bend
> To hold all love for creatures vain.

For when this love of God actually touches the soul, it finds no trouble in withdrawing from the love of creatures (I mean that the soul is not bound by any love for them), which is impossible without this divine love, for every strong love for creatures troubles us, and we suffer much more keenly if we must withdraw from them. When God takes possession of a soul, He gives it, by degrees, the empire over all created things even when He withholds the realization of His presence and His consolations, which is what you complain about. Although these disappear as though they had never been, as far as regards the sensitive faculties to which God was pleased to impart some of the joy of the soul, He does not quit the soul itself nor fail to leave it rich in graces, as is proved by the after effects.

Do not take any notice of the troubles which you tell me ensue. Although I have never experienced them myself, God having in His goodness delivered me from these passions, I believe they are caused by the intense delight of the soul stimulating the lower nature. With the help of God the trial will pass if you take no notice of it as several people have told me. The trembling will also cease. At first the soul is alarmed at this favor, as well it may be, but after receiving it several times, becomes better prepared for its reception. Do your best to resist the trembling or any other outward sign, lest it should become a habit, which would hinder rather than help you.

The heat which you mention is of no importance, doing neither harm nor good, although it might injure your health if it were excessive. It will probably cease by degrees, like the fits of trembling. As far as I can judge, such things are a matter of temperament; yours being sanguine, the strong mental emotion and natural heat which rise to the upper part of the body and the heart, may produce these symptoms. But as I said, the prayer is none the higher for them.

I think I explained about your feeling afterwards as though nothing had happened. I am not sure whether it is St. Augustine who says, "The Spirit of God passes like an arrow through the air, leaving no trace." I remember having answered this question, but I have received a pile of letters since you wrote, to many of which I have still to reply on account of want of time. On some occasions, the soul cannot return to itself for several days. Like the sun whose rays give warmth, although itself unseen, so the soul appears to dwell apart and to animate the body from outside, because some faculty is suspended.

Glory be to God, the kind of meditation you make when not enjoying the prayer of quiet is excellent.

I do not know whether I have replied to all your questions. As a rule I read through your letter again, which is no small advantage when I have time for it, but today I have only been able to refer to it piece by piece. Do not take such trouble with your letters to me; I never revise my own. If any letters in the words are missing, fill them in as I do with yours. One sees at once what the words were meant for and it would be loss of time to correct them.

I send you a hair shirt to wear when you cannot become recollected during the time of prayer, or when you feel anxious to do something for God. It will do much to rouse love for God, but I give it to you on the condition that on no account must you wear it after you are dressed for the day or when you sleep. You may wear it on any part of the body so long as it feels uncomfortable. I let you have it with misgivings, for your temperament is so sanguine that very little would affect your circulation: still, with such a love for God as yours, anything we do for Him, even such a trifle as this, gives such happiness that I did not like risking the trial. When the winter is over, we will try some other trifling thing of the sort, for I do not forget you. Let me know how you get on with this little plaything, for a plaything it is if, when we try to take some vengeance on ourselves, we remember what our Lord suffered. I laugh as I write, for you send me sweets, presents, and money, and I repay you with a hair shirt. . . .

Your Honor's unworthy servant,
Teresa de Jesus

Reflection

Prayer of Union: God proves His greatness by "upraising" the wretched. He favors them with ecstasies so intense they are embarrassing. He carries these miserable creatures outside themselves, making them burn to render more loving service even as they feel completely unworthy and unproductive. These exalted souls do not and cannot understand the excessiveness of love poured upon them. At the same time, all this favor does not dispose them to think they are any better than anyone else or that they are less in need of salvation than others. Instead, they are more vulnerable, more humble, more reliant on their neighbors and on each other. And in all this vulnerability and desire to do something beautiful for God, they have the courage to be joyful and at peace. Such are effects of the prayer of union, the highest degrees of mystical prayer to which we all ought to aspire.

St. Teresa has already allowed herself to be lifted into the highest degrees of prayer, and she writes her brother Lorenzo filled with confidence that he has also begun to taste a deeper union with God. It is out of this certitude that the great mystic consoles and counsels her brother. Although renowned for her holiness and spiritual doctrine, she does not present herself as a guru who has already arrived, but instead as a fellow pilgrim who is just a little further along on the same path.

Lorenzo is not a member of a contemplative community. He is not a priest or a religious. Don de Cepeda is, instead, a layman, a widower, and a loving father. A man of action, of proven courage and industry, this veteran Conquistador challenges the stereotypes that many might attribute to a pious mystic. Yet, having made his fortune in the New World and then returned to Spain, his saintly sister has raised his heart to higher things.

He is zealous in his efforts to pray, and has shared some interesting physical phenomenon. He has also begun to experience a certain absence of the Lord even as the fruits of his prayer appear to be good. It is into this experience of zeal and confusion, effort and absence, that St. Teresa speaks.

The great mystic opens up the beautiful paradoxes of mystical union. God "gives" "empire over all created things" when He "withholds" His Presence. His "absence" feels as though the consolation of His presence "had never been." Yet in this absence, the Lord "does not quit the soul itself nor fail to leave it rich in graces."

Instead of focusing on the physical sensations or sensible experiences of God's presence, Teresa recognizes and describes for her brother a very special grace, a beautiful work God has begun in him. Her passion is not the acquisition of spiritual experiences. Her heart is set on union with God. It is to a holy friendship with the Lord that she directs her brother. When she describes this new presence of God in him in terms of a "touch" and a "wound," she is simply speaking from her own experience into his experience. In her struggles to be completely free for the Lord, she learned how important it is to give her brother a word of hope. Her message is to see even his experience of the Lord's absence as the beginning of new and mysterious union with the Lord.

In this kind of prayer, that is, when we search for the Lord in the silence of our hearts even when He seems painfully absent, spiritual fruits abound and balance our affliction. One of these fruits is detachment.

Detachment as the Fruit of Prayer: The detachment St. Teresa celebrates is not a cold indifference to the gifts of God or the needs of our neighbors. Such indifference would never produce a letter like this beautiful reflection for her brother. Saints never fear implicating themselves in the plight of those entrusted to them by the Lord. Instead, they tend to be more concerned about their friends than their friends are for themselves. The Love of God gives them this spiritual liberty.

The detachment St. Teresa is proposing involves setting right the affairs of the heart. This interior integrity rests on the freedom to fully love the One who should be loved above all, and then to love everything else in relation to Him, for He is Love Himself. The seeming absence of this Presence of Divine Love is like a beautiful shadow that hides the soul from all kinds of misleading fantasies about God. Teresa proposes that an effect of this sacred darkness is a healthy separation from relationships and things that are not worthy of the divine friendship the Lord desires to share with us.

This kind of detachment takes the form a holy liberty to love whether in prayer or in action, in renunciation of comforts or the taking on of corporal discipline of some kind. Appreciating detachment as the freedom to truly and fully love helps us appreciate her counsel about her gift of a hair shirt. Still used today in some religious communities to help break an addiction to physical comfort, this inner clothing is very uncomfortable for the skin.

Ascesis: Unfortunately, this kind of physical asceticism can easily devolve into prideful self-abuse, especially when it is practiced while looking for measurable results. In the spiritual world, there is no cause and effect when physical methods are employed to get spiritual results. One cannot and must not presume that any spiritual practice produces, in itself, an increase of grace in the soul. Grace is a gift and such practices only dispose to this gift if they are done with the right loving disposition. This is why their use is discerned under the spiritual guidance of someone who is not overly fascinated with them. St. Teresa exemplifies, by her nonchalance, the sober common sense that is required in discerning corporal ascetical practices.

Welcoming the Gift of God is a matter of love and hospitality, not clever calculation. Thus, Teresa makes light of the hair shirt and is a realist about what its use can accomplish. In the spiritual liberty of the children of God, hair shirts and any other form of corporal asceticism are no more than toys, "playthings" not for self-abuse or results, but for love alone.

In this holy proportion between affliction and fruitfulness proposed by St. Teresa, we see the creative work of the Holy Spirit sanctifying our souls. When He permits an absence of sensible consolation during prayer, the Holy Spirit is allowing desires for lesser things to die. Our efforts at asceticism simply remove obstacles to this work to the degree they are informed by loving devotion and not by clever calculation. Only the Holy Spirit accomplishes this purifying work when He wants and how He wants. Just as it is beneficial for the growth of a vine when it is pruned, the mystical death to sin into which He leads creates space in the heart for more wondrous desires to be born and grow.

When we are faithful to the Lord in the prayer He has entrusted to us, His fruitful presence becomes new and unfamiliar in ways that are easily misunderstood and even unrecognized. Likewise, in our awareness of Him in prayer, He discloses Himself for our consolation according to our spiritual needs but not always in the ways we expect or desire. This is one of the reasons finding spiritual friendships and seeking spiritual direction is so very important if progress in prayer is to be made. What we think we want and what we think we understand needs to be discerned and sometimes renounced in the guiding light of a fellow pilgrim who has journeyed a little further ahead and can help us navigate the difficult topography of the way of the Cross. St. Teresa has more to say to her brother on this point, and we find this in her next letter to him.

DAY 27

CLXXII
Toledo. February 10, 1577[1]
To Don Lorenzo de Cepeda, Avila
Spiritual advice. Affairs of the order and Lorenzo's family.
Jesus be with your Honor.

I HAD recovered from my weakness of the other day, but seemed very bilious, and lest it should prevent my fasting in Lent, I took a purgative. However, I had so much to do and so many letters on the same day, that I was writing until two o'clock in the morning which gave me a severe headache. I believe that in the end this will benefit me, as the doctor has forbidden me to write after midnight and I am to employ a secretary sometimes. I certainly have been working too hard this winter for which I am much to blame, for I took time from my sleep in order to leave the mornings free, and as I wrote after my sickness, all conspired to injure me. Although I was very ill on the day I took medicine, I seem to be getting better. Do not feel anxious about me, for I take great care of myself. I mention it so that you should know the reason if you sometimes receive letters from me in another handwriting, or if they are very brief.

I look after myself as well as possible and was vexed at what you sent me, for I would rather you had eaten it yourself. Sweet things do not suit me, although I have taken some of this and shall again. But you must

---

1. Teresa of Avila, *Letters*, vol. 2, excerpts.

not send any more or you will annoy me very much. Is it not enough that I never treat you to anything sweet?

I do not understand about the *Pater Nosters* you recite while taking the discipline: I said nothing about them. Read my letter again and you will see. You must on no account do more than I advise: that is, take it twice a week. In Lent you may wear a hair shirt once a week, on the condition that you leave it off if you find it injures you, for you are so sanguine that I very much fear it will be bad for you. I cannot consent to your taking the discipline more often as it injures the eyesight—besides, it is a greater penance to moderate one's mortifications at first, which breaks the will. You must tell me whether the hair shirt makes you feel ill.

The peaceful prayer you mention is the prayer of quiet described in the little book.[2] The movements of your senses, as I told you, are to try you; I am convinced that they are of no account, and that it is best not to notice them. A very learned theologian once told me that a man came to him in great distress because whenever he received Holy Communion he was troubled with temptations against purity of a far worse kind than yours and had been told only to receive the yearly Communion which is of obligation. Although the theologian was not a spiritual man, he understood that it was a temptation and told the man to pay no attention to it but to communicate every week. When he lost his fear of it, the trial left him. You, too, must attach no importance to such thoughts.

You can consult Julian of Avila on all points, for he is very good. He tells me that he gets on well with you, of which I am extremely glad. You should visit him from time to time, and when you wish to do him a kindness give him an alms, for he is very poor and detached from money. In my opinion he is one of the best priests in Avila. Such society is good for us for we cannot be always at prayer.

As regards sleep, I advise, in fact I *order* you not to take less than six hours. Remember, we who are getting old must take care of our bodies

---

2. She is speaking of the Way of Perfection.

lest they should weaken the intellect, which is a terrible trial. You would not believe what misery I am suffering, for I dare neither read nor pray, though, as I said, my health is better. But I assure you, I shall take warning for the future. So follow my advice by which you will fulfil your duty to God. How foolish to suppose that this is the same prayer that kept me awake! There is no resemblance between them, for I made far greater efforts to go to sleep than to remain awake. I thank our Lord heartily for the favors He shows you and the good effects they leave. This proves His power, for you are left with virtues which you could not have acquired by prolonged efforts. Believe me, your brain exhaustion does not come from eating or sleeping too much, so obey what I tell you. Our Lord has shown me great mercy by giving you such good health. May He preserve it for many years so that you may employ it in His service.

The dread you experience is certainly produced by your spirit's realizing the presence of the evil spirit, and although you do not see it with your bodily eyes, your soul must either see or feel it. Keep some holy water near you; nothing drives the devil away more quickly. It has often stood me in good stead. Sometimes I have not only been seized with fear but have been terribly tormented as well.[3] Let no one know this. But the demon does not go unless the holy water touches him, so you must sprinkle it all around you.

Believe me, it is no small boon that you sleep so soundly: God gives you a great blessing. I repeat that you must not curtail your rest, for you cannot do so at your age.

It seems to me very charitable of you to be willing to bear trials and to leave consolations to other people: it is a great grace from God that you should even think of such a thing, though you are very simple and wanting in humility if you imagine that, without prayer, you could acquire such virtues as those which God has given to Francisco de Salcedo or to yourself. Trust my word and leave all to the Lord of life who

---

3. In her deposition for the canonization, Teresita declared that sometimes St. Teresa's head trembled and her body was covered with bruises from the blows given her by the devil.

knows which each of us needs. Never have I asked of Him interior trials though He has sent me very heavy ones during my lifetime. Such sufferings depend upon our constitution and humors. I am glad you are beginning to understand that saint: I want you to bear with his condition very patiently. . . .

I am your Honor's servant,
Teresa de Jesus

Reflection

Prayer of Quiet: The prayer of quiet is one of the degrees of mystical prayer that St. Teresa began to write about years before, but at this stage of her life she has begun to refine her discourse in meaningful ways. In the *Way of Perfection* to which she refers, she introduces some distinctions aimed at purifying and intensifying the effort of mental prayer. To this end, she proposes that the prayer of quiet is more than an initial movement of infused recollection but not yet an experience of full union. This prayer that prepares for a deeper union involves its own specific operations of the Holy Spirit in depths of the soul.

The prayer of quiet is an initial movement of mystical prayer but it has not yet attained to the mystical union which even higher forms of contemplation avail the soul. A pioneer in the renewal of mental prayer in the life of the Church, St. Teresa was convinced that there was a great difference between prayer acquired by one's own grace-filled efforts and prayer that is given as an infused mystical gift. Infused prayer always involves a deeper surrender to the Holy Spirit. Initially, however, one does not always catch when the shores of acquired prayer are drenched under the waves of the Gift of the Spirit.

This transition to prayer under the impetus of the Holy Spirit is recognized sometimes only after the fact. Souls that have progressed beyond initial impulses of the Holy Spirit in prayer look back and understand the new work that God has begun in them from their new vantage point. At the same time, as one makes progress from one grade of prayer to the next, especially from the ascetical grades of prayer under the direction of reason to the mystical grades of prayer led by the Holy Spirit, there are different kinds of counsels that apply. What worked well at one point in the spiritual journey no longer benefits the soul, and a new norm of conduct needs to be learned. These are often the most critical points for the pilgrim to seek spiritual direction.

St. Teresa is trying to help her brother understand a new rule for conduct that flows from the new kind of prayer he has been given. While prayer practiced under the command of grace-filled reason requires determination and perseverance, prayer under the impetus of the Holy Spirit involves a deeper trust and humble surrender before the presence of God. The reason for this shift concerns the very nature of mystical prayer as distinct from ascetical practices.

Lorenzo is accustomed to experiences in prayerfulness acquired not only through the recitation of prayers he learned by heart, but also through an acquired practice of recollection in God's presence. This acquired habit of prayer has inclined this layman to a deep silence and awe before the presence of God. His natural powers seem to be perpetually aware of the Lord's presence and ready to respond to Him. This is a normal, natural awareness healed by grace, but it is not yet the union with God that St. Teresa believes Lorenzo is being invited to share.

Unlike acquired states of prayer, states of mystical prayer, even the most initial, are not produced by any effort. Activity under the control of reason is inadequate for the total union of divine freedom and love with human freedom and love. St. Teresa is trying to help her brother understand that human effort, when aided by grace, serves only to prepare for this new work of the Holy Spirit. When the Holy Spirit begins to move in the heart, our efforts can even get in the way.

Lorenzo, on the contrary, is trying to produce a state of union through abusing himself whether by a lack of sleep, not enough food, a misuse of the discipline, or even the hair shirt about which she had already warned him. St. Teresa is rather pointed in discouraging him from his results-oriented approach. His heart is not surrendered in freedom to divine freedom. She discerns, in his self-mortification, little more than a misguided effort calculated to produce results it can never attain. Teresa is attempting to free her brother from a cycle of frustration and exhaustion that will not only endanger his health, but take him further and further from the heart of God.

The transcendent immensity of God's presence is not surmounted by titanic efforts at self-abuse or rash neglect. By virtue of having made Himself fully accessible through a simple movement of love revealed on the Cross, people of prayer like Lorenzo can only enjoy this access to the degree that they will also humble themselves. Not by the noise of her brother's self-reliance, but by the silent music of reverent surrender before Divine Mystery, God's vulnerability to humanity can manifest in him His surprising transcendence over His own absolute transcendence. It is this subtle work of holiness and of friendship with God that Teresa wants Lorenzo to know.

The prayer of quiet, like the initial experiences of infused prayer, is a fully divine work in the soul, but a much deeper and more beautiful one than the first movements of the Spirit. As the soul enters such a holy sanctuary, it can easily be distracted by its unworthiness. Rather than being anxious over impure thoughts, Teresa is advocating attention to the incomprehensible peace which God establishes in the soul.

In this deeper kind of silence, a new spark of holy fire ignites the soul, propelling it towards a union it has not yet known. The soul begins to enjoy an unfamiliar light and warmth sometimes augmented by touches and wounds of love ministered by the Holy Spirit. What He does in those moments infinitely surpasses all our efforts in not only a new fruitfulness but also the possibility of a new fruition that explodes into a new range of holy desires. All of this ignited interior intensity is a preparation for mystical union, grades of prayer in which intimacy with the Lord anticipates what awaits us in the world to come.

Lorenzo has taken up one act of devotion that Teresa does not discourage, and it is with this tender effort that we will conclude this reflection precisely because this effort is fully commensurate with what God is accomplishing in the prayer of quiet. The act of devotion that St. Teresa commends and that we also should linger over is also an act of mercy.

Don de Cepeda and St. Teresa of Avila know the holiness of their friend Francisco de Salcedo. They also know that he is not well and Lorenzo has made efforts to look after Francisco. She identifies them with one another, implicates them in suffering, in prayer, and holiness. She praises Lorenzo's ability to see the holiness of Francisco even in his present condition. After reminding him of the necessity and the primacy of prayer, she asks her brother to "bear" with Francisco "very patiently."

Our suffering in love makes us vulnerable to the unrepeatable and surprising ways He wills to be present and fruitful within the depths of hearts and in our relationships with one another. Thus, in each sacrifice and hardship we endure for love of God, there is always a new grace and a new kind of presence waiting to be enjoyed. Our delight in this divine radiance is commensurate to the patient love and prayer we take into these difficult ambiguities. Prayer alone helps us to face the dark hardships into which the love of God and neighbor calls us.

DAY 28

CCXX
Avila, March 26, 1578[1]
To Doña Maria de Mendoza
Consolation in trials.
JESUS!

MAY THE Holy Spirit ever be with your Most Illustrious Ladyship and give you strength to bear such trials, for you have indeed received a heavy blow, and I grieved deeply over your sorrow. Yet the favors that our Lord shows you convince me that He will not fail to console you in this sorrow and to recall to your memory what His Majesty and His glorious Mother suffered in this holy season. If we realize this as we ought, we shall bear all life's trials easily.

I should much like to be with you so that I might share your grief, though even here I have borne no light part of it. My only comfort has been to beg St. Joseph and our Lord to be with you. Besides our other prayers, we have not neglected to intercede for that holy soul, which I hope God has already taken to Himself, since, before it learnt more of the world's evils, He drew it to Him. All things pass so quickly that, if only our minds faced this truth, we could not weep for those who die and go to gaze on God, for we should rejoice in their gain.

As far as appearances go, I too was very sorry for the Count, but Godour minds faced this truth, we could not weep for those who die

---

1. Teresa of Avila, *The Letters of Saint Teresa*, trans. Benedictines of Stanbrook (London: Thomas Baker, 1922), vol. 3, complete letter. Hereafter: *Letters*, vol. 3.

and go to gaze on God, for we should rejoice in their gain.esides our other prayers Majesty watches over all your interests with special care, for He is a most faithful friend. Let us feel confident that He has considered what is best for souls—all else matters little in comparison. Eternal weal or woe is what signifies; so I beg of you, for love of our Lord, not to brood over your reasons for sorrow but to think about what is consoling. Thus you will gain greatly, but by the other course you would lose. Besides, you might injure your health of which you are bound to take care because of its importance to all of us. God grant you a long life as we beg of Him.

The sisters and the Mother Prioress kiss your hands repeatedly, as I do those of my señora, Doña Beatriz.

Today is Wednesday in Holy Week. I did not write before, thinking you would not wish for letters.

The unworthy servant and subject of your most illustrious Ladyship, Teresa de Jesus

Reflection

Suffering and Spiritual Progress: The wisdom of God and His secrets are only known by those who are open to the Holy Spirit. The Divine Consoler searches the heart of God and imparts this wisdom when we have been humbled enough to welcome it. The goodness and beauty that this wisdom instills is so great, it delights the heart of the Father. At the same time, our resistance and indifference to this great gift is only overcome with the heavy blows and disappointments God permits for this purpose. How do we help our friends when they are crushed by the sorrows the Lord permits them to suffer? It is a matter of being a good neighbor who will have the courage to stand with those we love before the inscrutable secrets of divine judgment.

"He is a most faithful friend." St. Teresa offers this encouragement to the prominent widow and a close friend of the reform. Dona de Mendoza has been a generous supporter of Teresa of Avila's work, not only financially but also spiritually. Her brothers, one a bishop and another a prominent political figure, have also been a great support through the years. Yet this benefactor and friend is here devastated by the early death of a loved one as well as other misfortunes.

In counseling her friend in regards this "heavy blow," it is important to note that St. Teresa grieves with her. She has allowed her heart to be pierced by her friend's crushed spirit. It is only to the degree that Teresa enters into solidarity with her friend's sorrow that she is able to reinforce the primacy of divine providence in a credible way. Otherwise, her words are no more than pious wishes, and such nice ideas never bandage wounds or provide shelter. To console another, to be a true neighbor, we must share their sorrow.

In the context of a shared sorrow, Teresa proposes that God is solicitous for her friend not in some general way, but in a very particular way, "with special care." The great Carmelite mystic is identifying Maria to be the recipient of the Lord's singular concern because He has implicated Himself with her in both sorrow and hardship by friendship. How does Teresa of Avila know this?

This loving knowledge of the Lord is the irreplaceable fruit of mental prayer, of contemplation in the heart of the Mystical Body of Christ. The heart of Christ is a place of intimacy and love, of tenderness and vulnerability, of truth and goodness. It is ready to be pierced by the plight of others, especially friends and neighbors, but even enemies. It has overcome every evil and proven stronger than death. The Church as the Mystical Body of Christ lives out of this deepest center implicated in every sorrow and every hardship.

In the Body of Christ, contemplatives know this heart because the life ordered around the pursuit of mental prayer penetrates into it, suffers its beautiful movements and searches its depths more than any other activity in the life of the Church. The greatness of this vocation and its singular importance account for why the contemplative vocation and mental prayer must remain a vital concern of every Christian. This vocation is dedicated to seeking, with love, the loving glance of the Lord. Although every Christian should make time each day for this pursuit, contemplatives who have left everything to find this pearl remain in the life of the Church a living sign of the Lord's faithful love, a love whose power is greater than death, a love whose mystery is not limited to this life.

Through her generosity over the years, Lady Maria de Mendoza witnessed to the responsibility of the whole Church to support the life of prayer. Concerned for St. Teresa and her nuns, she used her resources to protect and promote contemplation, this pursuit that seeks to gaze on Christ's mysterious presence. Because of her sacrifices and kindness, many were able to behold the loving look of the Lord that had years before converted St. Teresa. This glance at the love of Christ is what continued to motivate Teresa in the reform of prayer she took up through her Carmelite vocation, and it is this same love that now draws her into a real solidarity with Lady Maria de Mendoza.

"[The Lord] is a most faithful friend." This statement is not reducible to simply a nice thought or a polite thing to say. When we think about the circumstances in which these words were penned, they can only be taken seriously when regarded as a heroic act of faith. The great doctor of the Church has the power and confidence to propose this great truth because she is suffering its mystery in her own misfortunes and crushing blows.

At the writing of this letter, everything that could go wrong for both the reform and St. Teresa has indeed come to pass. Ecclesiastical authorities have misunderstood her efforts and she has fallen out of favor. Several weeks before she penned this letter, she broke her arm. Shortly after this physical mishap, St. John of the Cross was imprisoned by Carmelite friars in a secret location. People have lost confidence in Teresa and in her whole effort to renew the life of prayer in the Church.

In the face of all of this misfortune, this letter witnesses to how St. Teresa's confidence in the Lord's faithfulness is undaunted. When she counsels her friend not to "brood," Teresa is speaking out of her own experience. The trials that the Lord sends to us are impossible to bear if we will not maintain the discipline of living "by the love of God."

Teresa offers us a beautiful insight into what it means to live by the love of God in her specific counsel to "think about what is consoling," a wise echo of St. Paul's admonition in his letter to the Philippians:

Finally, brethren, whatever is true, whatever is honorable, whatever is just, whatever is pure, whatever is lovely, whatever is gracious, if there is any excellence, if there is anything worthy of praise, think about these things. What you have learned and received and heard and seen in me, do; and the God of peace will be with you. (4:8–9)

Choosing to find something truly consoling in the midst of great hardship is a fundamental disposition of contemplative prayer. Mental prayer searches the inexhaustible riches of Christ in every situation, and in this quest often discovers a deeper solidarity with the Lord, who is the only consolation that really matters. God sends his messengers to encourage us to look for Him more ardently, but ultimately He Himself wants to be our consolation.

Maria does not recognize how favored she is by God. She cannot yet see beyond the present sorrows that have crushed her heart. Her friend, however, is inviting her to raise her eyes to a more beautiful horizon, for she knows "God's judgments are wise and his secrets inscrutable."

DAY 29

CCLXVII
1579?[1]
To a Carmelite Nun
How to bear persecution.

. . . IN ORDER to profit and advance by means of persecutions and injuries it is well to reflect that God has been offended by them before I have. When the blow strikes me, He has already been offended by the sin. The soul that loves its Bridegroom ought already to have pledged itself to be entirely His and to have no will of its own, and if *He* bears with the injury, why should *we* resent it? Our only sorrow should be that God has been offended, for the soul itself is not directly affected but is only reached by the sensitiveness of the body which richly deserves to suffer in this world.

To die or suffer—this should be our wish.

No one is tempted more than he is able to bear.

Nothing happens except by the will of God.

"My father," said Eliseus to Elias: "you are the chariot of Israel and the driver thereof."[2]

---

1. Teresa of Avila, *Letters*, vol. 3, fragment. The autograph was in the convent of Guadalajara in the eighteenth century.
2. 2 Kings 2:12

Reflection

Patience and Perspective in Suffering: Carmelites root their heritage in the biblical experiences of Elijah. This solidarity finds in prayer the strength to confound the oppressive cultural, political, and religious forces of his day. Pure of heart, Elijah identified with the poor and lowly. Just as he unmasked the false devotion of his day and became a living symbol of true devotion to the Lord, St. Teresa directs one of her nuns to his secret. Teresa wants those who have dedicated themselves to the path of Carmel to choose this persecuted prophet as their spiritual father. They can be chariot and driver in the Church, they can be caught up out of the sight of this world, if they learn, as he did, to hear and live by the voice of God when they are under fire.

This letter was written during a time in which St. Teresa and many of those who were her closest friends were being dealt with in a very unjust manner. Ridicule, calumny, imprisonment, and torture were doled out to thwart not infidelity or sin, but the effort to return to a more disciplined life and a more fervent pursuit of mental prayer. The temptation to indulge in righteous indignation and resentment would have been very tangible, and the mother of the reform understood the importance of offering a word of truth that might help in this difficult battle.

Her words remind all of us that any endeavor we take for the Lord must be pursued in a manner that is in relation to who the Lord is and how He acts. Only faith makes such freedom possible, but such grace also needs to be chosen and acted upon, or it remains a nice wish that does not cost us anything. Love that does not cost is not love. If God loves patiently when He is offended, we must try to love in the same way.

Her message is not reducible to moralism or pious drivel, but instead stands on a powerful insight into the very nature of God. It sides with God's decision to patiently endure evil, to show that evil does not ultimately define the situations we confront in life. This is true even when the circumstances are offensive and oppressive. When we are patient with God's patience, we avail ourselves of a profound contemplation, a beholding of the victory of good over evil. This vision that divine patience knows is what the mother of the Carmelite reform wants us to share.

Evil, even that which others inflict on us unjustly, is not limitless. Its painful extent is limited, but, in contrast, a love that endures is a love that is unlimited and a love that triumphs over death. The fact that friendship with God and mental prayer open up a participation in this victory is the basis from which Teresa counsels patient faith in the love of God as the better pathway when we are under fire.

We do not know the designee of this letter. It is providential that this person remains anonymous, for it invites us to also be the recipient of this beautiful wisdom. Bearing injury is not merely for the great heroes of our faith, but is for the everyday followers of the Lord. Teresa does not excuse any of her nuns or spiritual children from this difficult contest.

She requires them to stand firm, not in a sense of resigned obligation, but with the joy of choosing to behold the glory of God. For St. Teresa, this divine standard does not admit of resentment: Just as God bears injury not grudges, so too should we renounce anything that is not worthy of the Lord festering in our hearts.

The divine standard points to the mystery of beatitude. A beatitude is a moment in which we act in pure human freedom, unimpeded by anything that is not worthy of human nobility. This kind of blessing always involves a decision, a movement of grace-filled freedom, a defining choice for God, for love, for the truly human.

This kind of choice implies renunciation: we cannot be patient if we torment ourselves with resentment. We must say no, we must disavow our propensity to brood over injuries, to replay painful scenarios over and over again. To choose to stand with God implies a refusal to stand in self-righteous indignation.

Such a simple loving movement of heart bears fruit beyond anything that any other action can produce. The fruit of a single moment of beatitude lasts forever, rippling through one's whole existence and extends to all others who are connected to that moment and that person. "Blessed are the Persecuted"—the very apex of Christian beatitudes—is what Teresa holds out to us through the vision of God she invites us to see in her words: "He bears with injury."

Profound and fruitful happiness awaits those who love the Lord and make the decisions to be like the Lord. Resentment and bitterness destroy the beatitude that might otherwise be ours in the midst of persecution. These preoccupations of heart dissipate our spiritual strength.

DAY 30

CCLXX
Avila, January 31, 1579[1]
To the Nuns Of Seville
Exhorts them to bear persecutions with resignation and joy. The Saint's grief at the calumnies uttered against Father Gracian by the two nuns.
JESUS!
May the grace of the Holy Ghost be with your Charities, my daughters and sisters.

I HAVE never loved you as I do now nor have you ever been so bound to serve our Lord as when He is granting you the great grace of sharing somewhat of His Cross and the extreme abandonment His Majesty experienced on it. Happy the day when you came to this place where such good fortune awaited you! I envy you immensely: it is the fact that when I heard of all these reverses (which have been fully described to me), of how they tried to drive you from the house, with other details, instead of regretting it, I felt immense joy within myself at seeing that, without your having crossed the ocean, the Master had enabled you to discover mines of eternal treasures. I trust in Him that these will make you very rich and you will share your gains with us here. I feel full confidence that, in His mercy, He will aid you to bear all your troubles without offending Him in any way. Do not be distressed because you feel your trials deeply, for our Lord wishes to teach you that you are not

---

1. Teresa of Avila, *Letters*, vol. 3, complete letter.

as strong as you thought you were when you longed for sufferings so ardently.

Courage, courage, my daughters! Remember, God never sends any one trials too heavy to bear, and He is with those in distress. Since this is certain you need fear nothing, but rely on His mercy, for He will bring the whole truth to light and we shall discover some of the hidden plots with which the devil has been trying to upset everything, which caused me more pain than your present crosses.

Prayer, prayer, my sisters! And now let your humility and obedience shine forth. Let no one outvie all your Charities, especially the former Prioress, in obedience to her who has been appointed as your deputy superior.

Oh! What a good opportunity for profiting by the good resolutions you made to serve our Lord! Remember, He often proves us to see whether our actions will carry out our resolutions and promises. Do honor to yourselves as daughters of the Virgin, and to your sisters, by the way in which you bear this severe persecution; do your best and the good Jesus will help you. Though He may sleep in the boat, when the storm increases He will quiet the wind. He wishes us to ask Him, and He loves us so that He is always seeking how to do us good. Blessed be His name for ever. Amen, amen, amen.

All our communities are praying much for you, so I trust that, in His loving kindness, God will soon bring matters right. Be of good cheer, for when we consider it, all we undergo for so good a God amounts to little, considering what He bore for us, for you have not even shed your blood for Him yet, and you are with your sisters, not in Algiers. Leave it all to your Bridegroom and you will see that, before long, the sea will swallow up those who war against us as it did King Pharoah, leaving God's people free and longing to suffer more, seeing what they have gained by it in the past.

I have received your letter and wish that you had not burnt the one you wrote before, as it would have been useful. Theologians say that you might have refused to deliver up my letters, but it is not of much importance.

God grant that all the blame may fall on me, though I have felt the penalties of those who suffered wrongfully as a heavy burden.

What pained me was to see, in the process of information drawn up by the Father Provincial, charges which I know to be utterly untrue, for I was at the convent at the time. For love of our Lord examine carefully whether any one made the statements through nervousness or by mistake, for nothing matters as long as God is not sinned against. But falsehoods and slanders too, grieve me deeply. I cannot believe the statements, for every one knows how upright and modest Father Gracian's behaviour to us has been and what help he has given us to advance in our Lord's service. This being the case, it is very wrong to bring such charges against him, however insignificant.

Have the kindness to say so to these sisters, and abide with the Blessed Trinity. May They have you in Their keeping! Amen.

The community here send you very kind messages. When the clouds have blown over, they hope to have a full account of the matter from Sister St. Francis. Remember me to the good Gabriela, whom I ask to keep happy, for I know how very keenly she must grieve over the way in which Mother Mary of St. Joseph has been treated. I feel no pity for Sister San Jeronimo if her desires are genuine: otherwise, I pity her most of all. Tomorrow will be the eve of our Lady of the Candles (Candlemas Day).

I should much prefer talking to Señor Garci Alvarez to writing to him, and as I cannot say what I wish in a letter, I am not sending him one. Remember me to those of the Andalusian sisters to whom you dare mention this letter.

Your Charities' unworthy servant,
Teresa de Jesus

Reflection

Standing Firm in the Face of Opposition: The Sisters of Seville are in the midst of great turmoil. Caught in the civil war between the Carmelites of the Ancient Observance and the Discalced Reform, this community was torn in two: their prioress was deposed, and another imposed in a mean-spirited game of power and control. Confusion and calumny cast a shadow over this new community. It was a time of great testing, a "severe persecution."

St. Teresa is emphatic in this letter, repeating "courage, courage" and "prayer, prayer" and "amen, amen, amen." Her appeal is passionate and tender, the cry of a maternal heart for her daughters. She speaks out of deep friendship, completely implicated in their plight, proud to stand with them, pleased with their faithfulness even when they have been crushed. She admits no defeat and makes no concession. She is mobilizing her forces instead, directing them towards tactical advantages, a commander who communicates a compelling strategy.

Her strategic goal is not of this world. Her tactics are counterintuitive. She does not direct a political or social attack on her foes. She does not promise sudden liberation from the oppressive forces of this world. Instead, she leads them into an entirely different kind of struggle and rallies them on a spiritual battlefield. She perceives what her sisters cannot yet glimpse under the burden of sorrow and dismay that seems to overwhelm them for the moment.

Rather than be limited by petty politics and rivalries, St. Teresa beholds that which is above, the greater reality, over which the present distress of the here and now has no authority or power. She invites her community to claim this victory that has already been won. Prayer is more powerful than politics; and, in severe trials, the greatness of our religion reigns.

In the annihilation of the security and familiarity on which they once relied, Teresa directs them to what does not change: the heavenly realities before which this world must bend its knee. Hers is a call to mental prayer, to contemplation, to a living from the depths of the heart in severe trial. It is not a retreat or an escape; it is standing firm on the love of God. It is confidence that grace-filled humanity has the freedom to see God and stand with Him—because no power on heaven or earth or under the earth can separate us from the love of God.

She leads like Moses because she, like him, has contemplated the burning bush. For her this encounter is the growth of the gift of mental prayer that has unfolded throughout her whole life and prepared her to write this letter at this time when this community needs words of hope and reason to be of good cheer.

What she offers is a vision of glory, for the God who has never forgotten the lowly and oppressed has not failed to remember her Carmelites. They are not slaves of the moment or defined by the humiliation of their present circumstances. Futility does not have the power to rob them of the meaning, the harmony, the relation that their devotion enjoys when it is rooted in the Bridegroom's devotion for them. Together, in the deep unity of prayer with all their sisters and their spiritual mother Mary, they do not suffer alone but through the present testing of their love they embody the new Israel. Not forgotten and especially chosen by God, they are on a journey out of slavery to the freedom to worship the One to whom they belong.

SPIRITUAL DIRECTION
᠍ SERIES ᠍

SOPHIA INSTITUTE PRESS

If this book has caused a stir in your heart to continue to pursue your relationship with God, we invite you to explore two extraordinary resources, SpiritualDirection.com and the Avila Institute for Spiritual Formation.

The readers of SpiritualDirection.com reside in almost every country of the world where hearts yearn for God. It is the world's most popular English site dedicated to authentic Catholic spirituality.

The Students of the Avila Institute for Spiritual Formation sit at the feet of the rich and deep well of the wisdom of the saints.

You can find more about the Avila Institute at
www.Avila-Institute.com.

Sophia Institute

Sophia Institute is a nonprofit institution that seeks to nurture the spiritual, moral, and cultural life of souls and to spread the Gospel of Christ in conformity with the authentic teachings of the Roman Catholic Church.

Sophia Institute Press fulfills this mission by offering translations, reprints, and new publications that afford readers a rich source of the enduring wisdom of mankind.

Sophia Institute also operates the popular online resource CatholicExchange.com. *Catholic Exchange* provides world news from a Catholic perspective as well as daily devotionals and articles that will help readers to grow in holiness and live a life consistent with the teachings of the Church.

In 2013, Sophia Institute launched Sophia Institute for Teachers to renew and rebuild Catholic culture through service to Catholic education. With the goal of nurturing the spiritual, moral, and cultural life of souls, and an abiding respect for the role and work of teachers, we strive to provide materials and programs that are at once enlightening to the mind and ennobling to the heart; faithful and complete, as well as useful and practical.

Sophia Institute gratefully recognizes the Solidarity Association for preserving and encouraging the growth of our apostolate over the course of many years. Without their generous and timely support, this book would not be in your hands.

www.SophiaInstitute.com
www.CatholicExchange.com
www.SophiaInstituteforTeachers.org

Sophia Institute Press® is a registered trademark of Sophia Institute.
Sophia Institute is a tax-exempt institution as defined by the
Internal Revenue Code, Section 501(c)(3). Tax I.D. 22-2548708.